May I Kill?

May I Kill?

Just War, Non-Violence, and Civilian Self-Defense

JEFFREY K. MANN

WIPF & STOCK · Eugene, Oregon

Wipf & Stock
An Imprint of Wipf and Stock Publishers
199 W. 8th Ave., Suite 3
Eugene, OR 97401

www.wipfandstock.com

PAPERBACK ISBN: 978-1-5326-5203-5
HARDCOVER ISBN: 978-1-5326-5204-2
EBOOK ISBN: 978-1-5326-5205-9

Manufactured in the U.S.A.   09/27/18

Dedicated to those whose lives involve facing violence
so others do not.

The nation that will insist on drawing a broad line of demarcation between the fighting man and the thinking man is liable to find its fighting done by fools and its thinking done by cowards.

—William Francis Butler

Contents

Introduction

Education without values, as useful as it is,
seems rather to make man a more clever devil.

—C. S. LEWIS

I enjoy a privileged life. I have been spared the exposure to violence that so many others suffer through. This is not to say that I have never been punched in the face or looked down the barrel of a gun, but I consider the experiences of others and recognize that my life has been one of tremendous privilege.

Many of the people in my life—family and friends—have not been so fortunate. They have served in combat operations where death was commonplace. Some have patrolled our communities and been the first responders to tragedies that we would prefer not to imagine. Others I know have been forced to confront violent gang members, corrupt police, and hired killers. The people in my life have survived assault, rape, and attempted murder. They have liberated a concentration camp, survived the Rwandan genocide, stopped murderers, and committed murders themselves.

My own life of privilege may seem normal to many readers, and those described above the exceptions, but that is not actually the case. Those of us living comfortable suburban lives, in first-world countries in the twenty-first century, who have free time to read books on ethics, are not living the lives of typical human beings. We are fortunate to be living when and where bloodshed is easily avoided. At the same time, we know that violence—even extreme violence!—could appear at our doorstep on any day at any time. When that happens, people are often unprepared. Not only are they physically and mentally untrained, but they are generally not ready for the ethical questions that arise. Can I shoot an armed intruder? Is such violence evil?

Must I try everything possible first, and only use violence as a last resort? In short, before you or I are thrust into a life-and-death situation, are we prepared to answer the question of whether or not we can kill?

The ethics of violence is often relegated to theoretical discussion and debate. Certainly, academic questions about nations going to war, pacifism, ticking time bombs, and preemptive military strikes are important to consider. If we are to play a productive role in our nations, advocating for or against specific wars or political policies, we should have a clear moral compass to help guide our convictions. Thomas Jefferson (1743–1826) famously declared, "An informed citizenry is at the heart of a dynamic democracy." Well-informed citizens with critical thinking skills are essential for the thriving of a nation, and so we have a civic duty to work through an ethic of violence before we start marching in the streets or writing letters to our elected officials.

The morality of killing is often addressed by those who are in the business of violence. Men and women whose daily reality involves facing potential violence need to work through their moral convictions quite thoroughly and concretely. Facing violent criminals, whether as an officer of the law, EMT, or social worker, requires tremendously challenging decision-making. The legality of one's acts is obviously important, but we moral creatures hear a calling above and beyond the law of the land. We must answer to that internal voice. After all, not everything that is legally permissible is morally good. Additionally, psychological consequences of certain actions do not disappear simply because an act is declared legal. A clear ethical barometer is important both in the moment and for what follows. With regard to those in military service, Ellis Amdur writes, "Given that war is hell, the fundamental moral question of a warrior is how can one maintain a moral code whilst not only living in hell, but required to do hellish things."[1]

Even those of us who are unlikely to encounter severe violence, or be tempted to use it ourselves, benefit tremendously from a coherent and informed ethical framework that addresses its use. At some point in our lives, we may be called upon to be a Good Samaritan. However, unlike in the Gospel story, we may not find the victim after his attackers have fled. They may still be in the midst of the assault. What will we do then? Are we justified to use violence ourselves? Do we call in others (e.g., the police) to carry out the violence for us? Do we witness to a moral ideal by avoiding the use of violence at all costs? That particular moment is the wrong time to start working through answers to these questions.

1. Amdur, *Dueling with O'Sensei*, 259.

Before continuing any further with this discussion of "violence," it may be helpful to clarify how I am using the word in this context. The word "violence" is actually more slippery than we might suspect. Academic debates continue to swirl around questions about what exactly constitutes violence. Are boxing, wrestling, and rugby violent? Are police officers violent when they forcibly restrain a person? Is the confinement of a criminal suspect violent? Some say that words can be violent—a claim heard more and more on college campuses lately—but then are we speaking literally or figuratively? Is the consumption of animal flesh an act of violence?

For those interested in such questions, John D. Carlson has an excellent summary on the topic, entitled "Religion and Violence: Coming to Terms with Terms."[2] Fortunately, for our purposes, we may use a rather general definition. Our concerns here are with those actions that most people consider violent, and only those directed toward other human beings. This book deals with the use of physical force to kill or cause significant physical injury to other human beings. We will leave aside combat sports, where participants enter an arena willingly, as well as psychological violence.

As stated above, a coherent and consistent ethical framework is necessary for our own decision-making, but it is also important for its effects on others. We often forget that our words and judgments influence others' moral decision-making. For the sake of their well-being, we should think before we speak. This is especially true for parents and teachers, and even more so for those who work in public ministry. Spouting off clichés and platitudes is tempting, but it can easily confuse rather than clarify moral reasoning. For example, Father John Dear, a well-known pacifist, argues that violence is "immoral, illegal, evil, and impractical."[3] I cannot help but wonder if he realizes that such a claim is not simply a prescription for his own behaviors, but a (remarkably harsh!) judgment of others. Would he have scolded or condemned the woman who grabbed her shotgun in the middle of the night to protect her children when a lynch mob rode up to her house? How does the young daughter of a police officer react to such a statement, or the old man who was drafted into the infantry during the Korean War? A meaningful ethic of violence must be well-informed and critically examined.

Regardless of where your values and beliefs lead you, it is important to know your moral principles, to have considered them judiciously, and be prepared to act on them at a moment's notice. With that in mind, let me

2. Carlson, "Religion and Violence," 7–22.
3. Dear, "To Kill or Not to Kill," 1:13:28.

suggest three additional reasons that everyone should work through their own ethics of violence.

1.) *A coherent position on the ethics of violence is important if one is to act well.* If our goal is to work toward greater peace and justice in our communities—whether local or global—we must study how best to achieve that. Coherent values and beliefs can bring about good results; muddled thinking breeds chaos. Too often we are left in the morass of pious platitudes.

The claim that fighting should be a last resort sounds reasonable. However, that ethical principle sometimes leads to greater problems, as was the case with Neville Chamberlain's appeasement of Hitler in the 1930s. The longer the delay, the more opportunities a dangerous enemy has to harm others, gain strength, and prepare to thwart any resistance.

On the other hand, too many people simply opt for "an eye for an eye and a tooth for a tooth." While we have not yet left the world blind and toothless, countless lives have been needlessly lost when pride and vengeance found their justification in this precept—just ask the Hatfields, McCoys, Capulets, and Montagues. While the Code of Hammurabi was designed to rein in disproportionate responses, the opposite often transpires. Proportionality is thrown out the window as the violence escalates. One nation responds to another's perceived injustice, noncombatants are targeted, communities remember, and a vicious cycle of violence is begun.

When an individual or nation holds to meaningful principles that carefully govern the use of violence, mistakes can be avoided and positive opportunities perceived. This does not mean that we will always get it right, as our critical reasoning is often betrayed by selfish desires. Moreover, there are situations that are so morally complex that even armchair commentators with the benefit of hindsight will not agree on what was right or wrong (e.g., the bombing of Hiroshima and Nagasaki).

Reasoned ethical principles do not ensure that we will always act in ways that bring about the greatest possible end. However, we do not make the perfect the enemy of the good. The more we think critically about the ethics of violence, the more likely the arc of the moral universe will bend toward justice.

2.) *A coherent position on the ethics of violence helps us deal with the personal consequences of violence.* A growing field of literature in recent years has dealt with the subject of "moral injury." When we act contrary to our own deeply held ethical standards, the negative effects on our mental well-being can be significant. An act that produces this type of "moral injury" is one which "transgress[es] deeply held moral beliefs and expectations."[4]

4. Litz et al., "Moral Injury and Moral repair in War Veterans," 695–706.

Much of this literature focuses on military personnel returning from combat operations, men and women who killed other men and women in a warzone.

Very often, moral injury results from a poorly defined, or ill-defined, set of ethical principles. In 2013, Marine Captain Timothy Kudo wrote an op-ed for *The Washington Post* entitled "I Killed People in Afghanistan. Was I Right or Wrong?"[5] His personal struggle with his (lawful) actions was compelling, but it was curiously set against a rather undeveloped ethical system. Whatever moral values and precepts Captain Kudo may take for his own, his efforts to come to grips with his actions after his time of service would certainly have benefited from a clear ethic before he headed overseas. We are better able to deal with moral injury when we understand ethics as a discipline—both in helping ourselves and others

During Operation Iraqi Freedom (2003), accounts of abused American prisoners-of-war made the headlines. Many people wondered if Americans should also ignore the Geneva Convention. An Army sergeant was asked by a CNN reporter if Americans would respond in kind. "The soldier looked at the reporter rather incredulously, and then responded with some force, 'Of course not. That's not who we are.'"[6] Whether or not this American soldier had a commanding grasp of just war theory, he knew his own ethical convictions—he had a clear sense of right and wrong as it related to his difficult work in a warzone. With the benefit of a moral framework, he had ethical resources to rely on while overseas. I suspect he was also better prepared for the psychological difficulties that many combat veterans face after deployment.

3.) *A coherent position on the ethics of violence avoids catastrophic delays.* When people are forced to respond to violence, one of the biggest problems they face is that they freeze in the face of danger. This deer-in-the-headlights inaction can be a result of different factors—fear, confusion, uncertainty. In these cases, just like the proverbial deer on the road at night, it can get you killed.

One reason that people freeze or hesitate in an emergency is because they are concerned that their actions may cross an ethical line. In films like "American Sniper" or "Eye in the Sky," we catch a glimpse of the horrifying ethical choices that people must make in the context of war, and must make in an instant. Can you shoot a child, or let her die, when the lives of multiple others are at stake? In the moment is no time to consider such questions for the first time. While a critical ethic of violence is no guarantee that mistakes

5. Kudo, "I Killed People in Afghanistan."
6. As in Johnson, *Ethics and the Use of Force*, 88.

will not be made, it does allow for more timely decisions. When the failure to act is as much a decision as acting, a coherent moral framework is of the utmost importance.

One important legal debate in the United States is whether one has a duty to retreat, if possible, when faced with a physical threat. If someone with a knife threatens to stab me on the street, and I have a pistol, must I try to run away?[7] Legal considerations aside, this is also a moral issue. Even if the law says I can "stand my ground," my own moral code might dictate that I should avoid unnecessary violence at all costs, and flee if I can. In that moment, however, is not the time for me to think it through for the first time. A needless delay, as I struggle with my conscience, could get me killed. Whether I pull the trigger or turn on my heels and sprint to safety, the sooner I do so the better—for everyone involved.

Peace, Justice, Shalom, Salam

In any consideration of the use of violence, we must ask a very important question: "To what end?" What is it, exactly, that we are trying to achieve? In response to a violent action, or the threat of one, the goal is not simply to stop the violence. That may be desirable, but it may not be sufficient. In the words of William Allen White (1868–1944), "Peace without justice is tyranny." Adolf Hitler wanted peace, an end to the fighting, after he invaded nation after nation. Every tyrant wants peace. The goal for which we struggle is not simply the absence of fighting; it must include the presence of justice.

The Hebrew conception of *shalom* encompasses much of this goal, where wholeness, harmony, and uprightness exist together. It is a complete peace. In Islam, the same word and idea is found in the Arabic *salaam*. We are to strive, not merely for the absence of fighting, but for the presence of justice and human dignity throughout the entire community. Moreover, "There can never be shalom only for some, because the word itself means fullness and wholeness."[8]

Unfortunately, we often think about the resolution to conflict in terms of "winning." We want to conquer our adversaries. The Swedish theologian and bishop Krister Stendahl (1921–2008) challenges us to think differently. "Salvation as Shalom. It is not a question about whether we win. It is healing. It is reconciling. It is redeeming."[9] There are times that evil people must

7. For the sake of simplifying things, we will imagine a situation in a public place, rather than one's home, so as to avoid considerations of the "castle doctrine."

8. Stendahl, *Roots of Violence*, 37.

9. Stendahl, *Roots of Violence*, 40.

be stopped for such healing and reconciliation to take place. However, the ultimate goal, or *telos*, should be kept in mind. If violence is to be justified, it must be in service of *shalom/salaam*.

Where We Go From Here

It is not my intention within the pages of this book to propose a specific ethic of violence, insisting on exact rules that everyone should observe. As we will see, people rely on different theories of ethics to make their moral decisions. They have diverse authorities on whom they rely and different rules that they try to live by. Rather, it is my hope that readers will come to think more clearly about their own moral reasoning and actions as they relate to violence and the creation of *shalom/salaam*. In these pages, we will consider the strengths and weaknesses of various arguments, along with their historical context, to shed more light on the viewpoints presented.

At the same time, this book is not simply a survey of various positions on the topic. It contains normative claims and arguments. Some of these, I recognize, the reader may reject. If the rejection of an idea comes about after an honest hearing and critical assessment of its merits and liabilities, then we have made progress. My goal here is not to persuade everyone to adopt my particular ethics. Rather, it is more critical and informed dialogue about the ethics of violence that I hope to foster

This book is divided into five parts, each of which contains either two or three chapters. Readers may decide to select sections of interest, or skip sections that seem less relevant to their interests. While this is possible, the material in later chapters does rely on concepts and theories laid out in earlier chapters.

In Part One, we begin by taking a look at moral reasoning itself, the discipline of ethics. How is it that we determine right and wrong? The three dominant theories in western discourse—deontology, utilitarianism, and virtue ethics—are treated first. This is followed by an examination of the different approaches to ethics taken in the East and the West. With this theoretical foundation in place, the application of moral reasoning to situations of violence becomes easier and clearer.

Part Two considers the ethics of nonviolence. First looking at pacifist traditions in the West, and then nonviolent traditions in the East, a critical lens is used to examine both the foundations for such beliefs and their practice in the world. From Quakers to Buddhists, we consider different models of nonviolence, their strengths and liabilities, and what a consistent principle of nonviolence might look like.

From nonviolence, we move to just war theory in Part Three. First, classical just war theory is presented. This is followed by an examination of how this theory developed over the past two millennia, the different moral principles that shaped it, and revisions that have taken place in the modern era.

Following the presentation of just war theory, Part Four considers how this model can apply to situations of civilian self-defense. Here we delve into ethical dilemmas that civilians may face at some point in their lives, when compelled to act in the defense of themselves or others in their communities. Using the criteria of just war theory, it is easier to perceive the ethical dimensions of such situations and think critically about morally responsible action in response to them.

Finally, Part Five examines how morally virtuous behavior is not simply a function of a decision of the will. If one wishes to cultivate *shalom/salaam* in one's community, it is absolutely necessary to cultivate oneself as an entire person. Looking at the cultivation of the person in body, mind, and spirit, this final section considers what is necessary to become a person who is capable of acting with good intent, knowledge, and skill. The focus in this final section remains primarily on the context of civilian self-defense, although the principles clearly apply to those working in law enforcement or the military as well.

PART ONE

Moral Reasoning

Critical intelligence is a prerequisite of justice.

—Reinhold Niebuhr

In this examination of ethics, we begin with the assumption that the people involved have a genuine desire to be morally upright. Ethics does not ask whether you will do the right thing—that is a question for psychologists, I suppose. Ethics asks what the right thing to do is. Sometimes the answer to ethical questions is easy, but many times it is not: I know I should help my uncle clean his gutters when I visit him next month, but should I share a beer with him when I know he has a drinking problem?

This book assumes that the reader is interested in doing the right thing when it comes to matters of violence. The challenge is determining what behaviors are morally virtuous and which are not. There is not a single approach to this problem, but rather a variety of theories that people use to figure out how they should act. Even though most people cannot name and define a specific ethical theory, we all use various models on a day-to-day basis. Therefore, it is helpful to establish categories of ethics. This allows us to recognize the moral reasoning we currently practice, to do it better, and to understand how others reach their own moral conclusions.

The first chapter introduces three dominant theories of ethics: deontology, utilitarianism, and virtue ethics. We will examine how these methods attempt to determine what is morally right. We will also consider their shortcomings. With a basic understanding of these theories, we are in a much better position to engage the following question: "When, if ever, is violence justified?"

Determining the right course of action is not as easy as plugging in the particulars of a situation and waiting for the ethical theory to tell you the answer. Consider the question of the death penalty (which is not within the purview of this book). It is often argued that capital punishment is immoral because one of the Ten Commandments is "Do not kill." Others argue that this practice should be banned because it does not actually deter crime, pointing to the correlation between high crime rates and states that practice execution. There are also those who simply stick a bumper sticker on their car that reads "Death Penalty: What Would Jesus Do?"; this method suggests we should follow the nonviolent model of the Messiah.

These three arguments represent the three ethical theories mentioned above. However, the arguments are all flawed: the commandment opposes murder (i.e., the killing of an innocent), not executing a criminal; high crime rates could indicate that the death penalty is not a deterrent, or that states with high crime rates are more likely to adopt the death penalty (correlation does not equal causation); following the virtuous example of Jesus is often a good idea, but there is a danger in pulling him from history and declaring what position he would take on a contemporary moral issue.

This is not to say that the death penalty is a good thing. After all, there are plenty of faulty arguments in support of it. The point is that there are moral arguments out there, grounded in different ethical theories, which sound good but do not hold up under scrutiny. This book intends to supply the tools to aid in the analysis of moral arguments about violence. In order to make coherent arguments, determine what is morally right, and recognize the value (or lack thereof) in others' opinions, it is crucial to understand ethical theory. So, let us begin.

CHAPTER 1

Ethical Theories

A man without ethics is a wild beast loosed upon this world.

—Albert Camus

Deontology

Deontology, or deontological ethics, is ethics based on following certain absolute and universal moral rules. For this reason, it is often described as "rule-based" ethics. If you follow universal rules that tell you which behaviors are morally right and which are morally wrong, then you are likely engaged in deontological ethics. One subcategory of deontology, found more commonly in the West, are commands from God. This is a type of deontology known as *Divine Command Ethics*.[1] The Ten Commandments were given by Yahweh to Moses on Mount Sinai; they are commands from God and are therefore universally valid for Jews and Christians and should always be followed. Christians believe that Jesus is divine—the incarnate second person of the Trinity. When he tells his followers to visit the imprisoned, turn the other cheek, or follow the Golden Rule,[2] they are being given an ironclad rule that should be relied upon and followed in all ethical dilemmas. The Koran was transmitted from Allah to the Muslim people

---

1. Not all ethicists consider divine command ethics to be deontology. I belong to the camp that believes that they should be treated as such, but the reader should know there is professional disagreement on this matter.

2. "Do unto others as you have done unto you" (Luke 6:31; Matt 7:12).

and likewise contains divine commands for how to live your life. Following these rules is a moral imperative for Muslims.

In a nutshell, divine command ethics teaches that "God commanded it, so do it." In many respects, these ethics are easy to understand and follow, although there are concerns as well. Foremost is the question that people must ask: "How do I know this command is really from God?" We will not be trying to answer that question here, but the reader should be aware that such a challenge must always be faced by people following divine command ethics.

Non-Western religions have far fewer divine command ethics, as their religious traditions generally do not emphasize scriptures that are understood to contain God's moral rules for human beings. There are possible exceptions, like *The Law of Manu* in Hinduism, which allegedly contains the words of the god Brahma, but this approach to ethics is far less common in the East.

Most of the time, however, ethicists are not thinking about divine commands when they talk about deontology. (In fact, many philosophers do not even acknowledge divine command ethics when discussing deontological ethics.) For example, Thomas Jefferson insisted that everyone has certain rights—among them life, liberty, and the pursuit of happiness—in the Declaration of Independence. These human rights are unalienable and endowed by our Creator; we know about them because they are self-evident, not because the Bible tells us so.[3] Respect for these rights is then a moral imperative, and thus an example of deontological ethics.

Plenty of the world's greatest thinkers taught something called the Silver Rule,[4] or the Law of Reciprocity. Its most familiar formulation is, "Do not do unto others what you would not have done unto you." It has been expressed different ways at different times. In *The Analects*, Confucius (551–479 BCE) instructed his students "Never do to others what you would not like them to do to you."[5] Roughly a century before him, in Ancient Greece, Thales (c. 624–c. 526 BCE) taught, "Avoid doing what you would blame

3. Jefferson was not a Christian, but a deist. He believed in a God who created the world, but does not get involved in its daily business. Thus, there are no divine commands sent from above. We use our reason to attain knowledge of what is right and wrong.

4. There are those that see the Silver Rule ("Don't do unto others") as an alternate expression of the Golden Rule ("Do unto others"). From a purely logical standpoint, a case can be made for this. However, the spirit and intended principle of these different rules leads me to categorize them as different ethical precepts.

5. XV.24. This translation, from Arthur Waley, is found in XV.23, for some unknown reason.

others for doing." Still today, this is one of the most popular and persuasive deontological ethical principles throughout the world.

As already stated, deontology does not have to be religious at all. The great philosopher Immanuel Kant (1724–1804) taught the categorical imperative, which is the classic example of deontological ethics. Its first formulation reads, "Act in such a way that the maxim of your actions could be willed as universal law." That is, when you are choosing what to do in a moral dilemma, it should be possible to will the principle that governs your actions be followed by everyone. For example, is it okay if you take a single grape from the grocery store? The maxim of your actions would be stealing, and it is impossible to will a world in which people could steal whenever they want to. So, do not take the grape. In other words, never make an exception for yourself when it comes to moral quandaries.

Kant's categorical imperative is not treated at length here, but this is not because of any lack in its importance. It is the quintessential example of deontology. However, the following chapters will draw more upon religious deontology than Kant. This may be regarded by some as a shortcoming in my arguments, but the history of pacifism, just war theory, and popular ethics are grounded more in theology than Kant.

There are a few problems with the various schools of deontology. One is the difficulty of establishing that any absolute moral principle is, in fact, true. Was the divine command really communicated by God or simply created by some well-meaning individual? Do human beings really have unalienable rights to life, liberty, and the pursuit of happiness (let alone rights to work, leisure, and healthcare insurance), or are these just privileges that we decide to give one another to make our society a nicer place to live?

Second is the fact that deontology is very rigid, and we would really like to have more flexible rules to live by. Am I really not allowed to lie? Ever? Imagine that you were one of the noble individuals who hid Anne Frank and her family during the Nazi occupation of Holland. If your actions were discovered, not only would the Frank and van Pels families be shipped off for execution, but so would you and your family. If it happened one day that an eight-year-old boy stopped you on the street and asked if you were hiding someone in your attic, as he had seen shadows and heard noises while playing in the area, would you be morally bound to answer him truthfully?

The third problem is that it is not always so easy to understand what the moral imperative means. Jesus said "turn the other cheek," but does that mean we always do this? Are we supposed to be pacifists? The Koran prescribes the death penalty for murder "and spreading corruption [*fasad*] in the land." That could mean piracy or treason, but others have understood it to include extortion or drug dealing. It is not an easy task to determine how corrupt an action must be before it is *fasad* and therefore merits execution. Simply having a fixed rule does not mean everyone will understand its application in the same way.

Utilitarianism

Utilitarianism is an ethical theory that is often placed under the umbrella of consequentialism. For a utilitarian trying to figure out the right thing to do in a moral dilemma, it is the consequences of one's actions that matter, rather than obeying a fixed rule. This is often described as trying to create "the greatest good for the greatest number." Utilitarians also talk about creating "maximum happiness," but this does not simply mean making people smile and filling them with warm fuzzies. Happiness must be understood broadly in terms of human thriving or flourishing, as in the Greek concept of *eudaimonia*.[6]

One classic example of a moral dilemma that shows the difference between a utilitarian and deontologist is the "ticking time bomb" scenario. In this hypothetical situation, authorities catch a terrorist who has planted a time bomb in the city. The ethical question is whether or not it is acceptable to torture the terrorist in the hope of finding out where the bomb is before time runs out. While the deontologist is likely to insist that you cannot violate the rights of the alleged terrorist, even if it means thousands might die, a utilitarian is more likely to argue that torture is justified. According to this line of thinking, it is better to torture one terrorist than to allow the bomb to kill thousands of innocents. The action with the potential to create the greatest good for the greatest number seems clear in this case.

The crucial mistake, which is often made, is to assume that utilitarians all agree on what must be done. Any statement that begins, "*The* utilitarian position is" typically betrays a poor understanding of this theory. In the time-bomb scenario, a utilitarian may insist that the terrorist *not* be tortured. There are some very compelling utilitarian arguments for this: the likelihood of the terrorist responding to torture and revealing the true location of the bomb is minimal; this act of torture would establish precedent, resulting in an increased use of torture within our own country, among our allies, and certainly among our enemies; the moral status of our country

---

6. John Stuart Mill's *eudaimonistic* utilitarianism "defines happiness in terms of certain types of higher-order pleasures or satisfaction, such as intellectual, aesthetic, and social enjoyments . . . (e.g., high culture, scientific knowledge, intellectuality, creativity, and spirituality)" (Pojman, *Ethics*, 110).

would be diminished in the eyes of the world; such an act would rally our enemies and would be an effective recruiting tool in their hands. These considerations are other possible consequences to which a utilitarian might point, making an argument against torture.

The tension between the noble deontologist and the practical utilitarian makes for great drama, and we have seen it play out repeatedly in movies and TV. A conflicted but principled character—e.g., Jack Bauer or Jason Bourne—is caught between these two theories as time is running out. Fortunately, in such fictional accounts, a third option often presents itself so that the day is saved in a way that satisfies viewers of differing ethical convictions.

Utilitarians are often divided into two subcategories: the act-utilitarian and the rule-utilitarian. The former examines moral dilemmas, while asking which action will create the greatest good for the greatest number in a particular situation. The latter attempts to establish and abide by rules that will maximize happiness in the long run. For example, we can imagine cases wherein allowing freedom of the press would create more suffering. The rule-utilitarian, however, would likely insist that when we always abide by a freedom of the press, we achieve the greatest good in the long run. So, even if it may hurt more than it helps sometimes, we are better off always following such a rule, or respecting such a right. It is for this reason that rule-utilitarians can be strong advocates of fixed rules and human rights.

The fundamental problem with utilitarian ethics is simple: we don't know the consequences of our actions. We make guesses. Hopefully we make educated guesses. Unfortunately, we are often wrong. People tend to overlook relevant information and have plenty of biases. Even when we are well-meaning, we cannot forget the law of unintended consequences. As the saying goes, "The road to hell is paved with good intentions." When it comes to employing utilitarian ethics, we often make decisions that lead others into great suffering.

In the 1990s, many people in the United States became aware of the slave trade that was happening in Sudan. Stories of the refugee "Lost Boys," who escaped the slave trade, were making news around the world. Many people met the lucky ones who found asylum in countries like Australia, Canada, and the United States. Folks started to care deeply and sincerely about the plight of these black African men and women who were being enslaved by the Arabs who controlled the country. As a result, individuals and churches decided the right thing to do was to liberate as many Sudanese as possible from slavery. They raised funds, sent them to Sudan and Kenya with trusted representatives, and arranged to purchase the freedom of these slaves.

No one could doubt the integrity and good will of these generous do-nors, but they likely did more harm than good. In a nutshell, this approach increased the demand for slaves by the liberators' willingness to pay for them. The sale of slaves became more profitable and so there was a greater incentive for the local Sudanese to procure more slaves. The philanthro-pists wanted to achieve a greater good for a greater number of people, but through their failure to understand basic economics they may have made the situation worse.

While we can become better at predicting the consequences of our ac-tions, we cannot do so perfectly. I wonder how often we think we are doing the right thing and making the world a better place, while actually achieving the opposite. There are times in life when we encounter some jerk starting trouble. Perhaps he pushed, shoved, and threatened us—or some other per-son—for no good reason. For some of us, in a situation like this, we want to "teach this guy a lesson." In our own minds, we are doing something good: I get to stand up for the innocent, let him and others know this behavior is unacceptable, maybe deter similar actions in the future, and feel awesome for being a champion of justice. This is utilitarian reasoning. In reality, the beatdown he gets could push him over the edge, and he could return with a gun. He might go home feeling emasculated and compensate for it by beating his wife and children. There is also the very real possibility that in the process of "learning his lesson," he could fall and hit his head on a curb and die. (It happens more often than you realize!) In such a case, with one person dead and another spending a decade or two in prison, we would be pretty far from the greatest good for the greatest number. How would things really play out? Who knows?

None of this is to say utilitarianism is flawed. However, one must be cognizant of the fundamental difficulty in this approach to moral decision-making; we are guessing at consequences. If one is to adopt such an ethical approach to decision-making, there is a strong moral obligation to think critically and thoroughly about possible consequences. In any moral di-lemma, we must research the issue carefully, look at other precedents, ex-amine the data, consider psychology and economics, and propose a best course of action with enough humility to recognize possible mistakes in our judgment.

Virtue Ethics

While the utilitarian seeks the greatest consequences, and the deontologist adheres to absolute moral demands, the virtue ethicist is concerned with their character as a human being. Virtue ethics is an approach to moral deliberation where one looks to character for guidance more than the consequences of an action or fixed rules of conduct. Personal qualities (e.g., prudence, justice, restraint, courage, and wisdom) are the touchstones for determining proper behavior. Rather than ask about rules or consequences, actions follow from cultivated virtues. For example, drunkenness is not consistent with restraint, cheating is not compatible with justice, and disrespect for parents is not an act of filial piety. Louis P. Pojman (1935–2005), former ethicist at the United States Military Academy, sums up virtue ethics nicely. This approach "emphasizes *being*, being a certain type of person who will no doubt manifest his or her being in actions or nonaction. For traditional duty-based [deontological] ethics, the question is 'What should I do?' For virtue ethics, the question is 'What sort of person should I become?'"[7]

Virtue ethics has a long history. We find the cardinal virtues of "wisdom, courage, temperance, and justice" in Plato's *The Republic*, from where they may have found their way into later Jewish scriptures. Christians added "faith, hope, and charity" to the four just-described. Today, Western religious traditions (i.e., Judaism, Christianity, and Islam) are still influenced by the virtue ethics of the Greeks.

This approach to ethics is not limited to the western hemisphere. East Asian countries have a long history of influential virtue ethicists. Kong Fuzi, better known in the West as Confucius, greatly influenced China, Korea, and Japan. Confucius's teachings have directed emperors and peasants, the elderly and children, generals and laundry women, how to conduct themselves with one another in society. To do so, Confucius did not write volumes of canon law, detailing good and bad behavior. His approach was to describe what kind of person each of us should be.

In his *Analects*, he repeatedly describes the conduct of a "gentleman" or "good man," often contrasted with the "small man." He did not give his students a list of virtuous behaviors, but described what sort of people they should become:

> A gentleman can see a question from all sides without bias. The small man is biased and can see a question only from one side. (II.14)

> A gentleman takes as much trouble to discover what is right as lesser men take to discover what will pay. (IV.16)

---

7 Pojman, *Ethics*, 160.

The good man does not grieve that other people do not recognize his merits. His only anxiety is lest he should fail to recognize theirs. (I.16)

In addition to such descriptions of how a virtuous person behaves,
Confucius spent considerable time addressing the relationships that exist
in society. The five most important are as follows: ruler–subject, father–son,
husband–wife, elder brother–younger brother, and friend–friend. He firmly
believed that members of a society must know how to interact with one
another; they must know their place, responsibilities, and obligations within
society. When this is the case, a community can thrive.

Students of Japanese martial arts often learn the dojo *kun*, or the
statement of moral principles expected of all practitioners. My friend and
former training partner Hideyuki compared them once to the Ten Commandments, and there are indeed commonalities. However, a look at these
"rules" points to an important difference as well. At Hideyuki's dojo, the *kun*
includes these five directives:

1. Work to perfect your character.

2. Always act with good manners.

3. Refrain from violent and uncontrolled behavior.

4. Cultivate a spirit of endeavor and perseverance.

5. Have fidelity in seeking a true way.

What we do not find here are specific rules or regulations. The Ten
Commandments tell you to not lie, commit adultery, covet, murder, etc.
This stands in contrast to the *kun* above, which describes virtuous character,
not particular acts.[8] The *kun* tells you what kind of person to be, while the
Ten Commandments tell you what actions to practice or avoid.

With virtue ethics, a clear example of its strength is its flexibility.
Concrete rules, while often easy to understand and implement, can provide
difficulties in unusual situations. We are told, "Do not lie." Yet we wonder
if that is good advice when an extremely agitated woman holding a meat
cleaver comes to the door and asks, "Is your cheating, no-good roommate
home?" Virtue ethics direct us to be people whose lives are characterized by
values such as humility, compassion, and integrity. With these guiding principles, we have freedom to respond to the difficult moral dilemmas we face
with creativity and resourcefulness, rather than slavish devotion to rules. In
our day, when the credibility of universal moral rules is often questioned,

---

8. The commandment to honor father and mother may be closer to virtue ethics,
but the general trajectory of the Decalogue is clearly toward specific moral commands.

and utilitarianism can appear cold and calculating, there is a real attractiveness within virtue ethics.

At times, though, different virtues can come into conflict with each other. This may create moral confusion. For example, consider Confucian ethics, where filial piety (your moral responsibility to your family) and civic duty (your moral responsibility to your ruler or government) are paramount. What happens when these come into conflict? If you discovered your father had committed murder, would you turn him in to the authorities?[9]

Different cultures (and different people) have emphasized one virtue over another. In China, filial piety takes precedence over civic duty, while in Japan this is reversed. One can see this illustrated in the stories of Hua Mulan and the forty-seven *ronin*.[10] Chinese Mulan lies to the authorities and violates all sorts of laws and social customs in order to save her father's life. The forty-seven Japanese *ronin*, on the other hand, give up their lives to avenge the honor of their lord, knowing full well that their acts will leave their children fatherless, their wives widows, and their families destitute.

The strength of flexibility in virtue ethics, discussed above, is also a fundamental weakness. We turn to ethics to help us make difficult choices in the midst of moral dilemmas. Being told to respond to a situation with wisdom, compassion, or filial piety does not answer all of our ethical questions. When does human life begin? Does euthanasia respect the dignity of human life or deny it? Do human beings have a fundamental right to privacy? We are going to need more than cultivated prudence, courage, and charity to work through these ethical conundrums. People of strong and virtuous character will disagree as to the answers to these questions. We see, then, that the flexibility of virtue ethics can be both its greatest strength and weakness.

With a basic understanding of these three theories of ethics—deontology, utilitarianism, and virtue ethics—we can begin to do some application. When is violence justified? How much violence is justified? And, are my actions making the world a better or worse place?

The first two questions are not only moral, but legal. There is, of course, a great deal of overlap between morality and the law. Both prohibit murder, theft, and unnecessary harm to another, among many other iniquities.

---

9. Confucius, by the way, would tell you in no uncertain terms that you should not turn in your father.

10. The story of Mulan is quite familiar to Western audiences, thanks to the 1998 Disney film. The story of the forty-seven *ronin*, depicted in the Japanese tale entitled *Chūshingura*, as well as the 2013 fantasy film by Universal Studios, is the true tale of how forty-seven samurai avenged their feudal lord's death, knowing that they would all be required to commit ritual suicide (*seppuku*) after "justice" had been served.

However, among people for whom questions of morality are important—even essential to their lives—there is more at stake than simply avoiding illegal behavior. This is where the third question enters. Morality holds us to a higher standard than the law. The law does not prohibit swearing at my mom, but morality does. The law might permit me to stand my ground in a certain situation, but my ethical convictions might not. On the other side of the coin, there are those situations where the law prohibits something that morality may require me to do. Such occasions are quite rare—not nearly as common as many people imagine—but they do exist. We will consider some in later chapters.

As we consider questions related to the ethics of violence, readers may reach different answers. Some of this will depend on which ethical theories are (more or less) operative for the individual. Religious convictions are also a major factor in one's ethical reasoning. While I make arguments for certain positions in this book, I understand that people of good will and intellect may disagree. That's fine. The point is to clarify our thinking on these questions, not necessarily come to consensus.

CHAPTER 2

East vs. West

We are what we repeatedly do. Excellence, then, is not an act, but a habit.

—ARISTOTLE

It is possible to find deontology, utilitarianism, and virtue ethics in both Eastern and Western cultures. Between the two of them, these theories often look a little different from one another, and have different emphases, but they are not wholly dissimilar. There is, however, one significant distinction between eastern and western ethics that is worthy of note: the relative importance of pursuing the moral ideal. In the West, moral ideals are generally universal and everyone should strive to live by them. In the East, the expectation is not usually present that everyone will make an effort to live by the ideal. The foundation for this difference is found in a particular religious belief that often differentiates East from West: reincarnation.

The major Western religions of Judaism, Christianity, and Islam have all taught that human beings have one life to live on this earth, and that's it. Christianity and Islam both stress that, after this life, we all face our Maker and must account for what we have done. The righteous will inherit eternal life, while the unrighteous will be cast out.[1] As a result, it is extremely important that one get things right during this lifetime. There are no second chances.[2]

1. What constitutes righteousness and how it is attained (faith? good works?) is a subject of disagreement among these traditions, and not our concern here.

2. There are exceptions, for example in Mormon theology, but these are not the

The majority of Eastern religions have a shared belief in reincarnation (or rebirth). This lifetime is only one in a sequence of many thousands. We have had many lives before this one, and we will likely have many more to follow. Most people who believe in a traditional notion of reincarnation are not concerned with reaching the ultimate goal of human existence (reunification with the divine or nirvana) during this life. Rather, the concern is more about living a good life and achieving a good rebirth. Thus, there is less concern with getting everything absolutely right in this life, and more with doing a good job in one's individual circumstances. Most Hindus and Buddhists do not concern themselves with final liberation from this cycle of reincarnation; that can wait for a future lifetime of prodigious religious devotion. This time around it is enough to do well and be reborn under good circumstances.

The implication for ethics is highly significant. In the West, actions are either right or wrong. (This is reinforced by the West's preference for deontology.) You should do that which is right and avoid that which is wrong, period. Of course we often fail in our efforts, but the rule is universal and always binding. These moral precepts apply to everyone and we should all do our best to live accordingly.[3] We should not make exceptions for ourselves, regardless of the situation or circumstances.

It is true that Western religions place great importance on the mercy of God, forgiving the sins of those who are truly penitent. However, while God may forgive the sins of the believer, this does not change the absolute and universal nature of the moral precepts that have been established. The rules always stand. Sin is always sin—even when a merciful and beneficent God can forgive that sin.

With its belief in reincarnation, the East tends to look at things differently. Morality exists on a continuum of virtue. It is not about getting things absolutely right, but striving for higher levels of virtue. After all, one does not have to meet the ultimate standard in this particular lifetime to avoid eternal damnation and be assured an eternity in God's presence. What is important is to make spiritual progress, lifetime to lifetime. Living a good life is sufficient to ensure a good reincarnation. Therefore, not every moral ideal must be pursued, not every rule followed with exactness.

We can see this with the example of vegetarianism. While the moral ideal is not to eat meat, it is understood that vegetarianism is a luxury of the

norm.

3. The exception to this may be religious orders in Catholicism, where members take a vow to observe additional moral precepts. Hence, it is not wrong for lay Catholics to own property and have sexual relations with their spouses, but the "religious" pursue a higher moral calling of poverty and chastity.

wealthy. If your family is malnourished, and someone gives you a chicken, you eat the chicken. Doing so may not be in accord with the absolute moral ideal of never harming a sentient being, but in these circumstances vegetarianism is not a viable option. No one will condemn the man who slaughters a chicken to save his children. Perhaps in his next life he will have the resources to live without the consumption of meat.

The same is also true in less dire circumstances. Several years ago I had a conversation with a Sikh about vegetarianism. (Sikhism is another religion that teaches reincarnation.) Orthodox Sikhs believe that it is improper to eat meat. According to my friend, there are circumstances that have "so far prevented me from practicing the religion fully (besides, I love the taste of a Big-Mac or a Sunday pot roast!)." Thus, at this point in his life, he may not be particularly religious and concerned with the ultimate goal of human existence. Meeting moral ideals can wait until that time, or lifetime, when it becomes a priority.

While adherents of these Eastern traditions accept the legitimacy of the ethical claim, not everyone is expected to abide by the letter of the law. What is more important is making moral progress, not getting everything right. As we will see within Hinduism and Buddhism, nonviolence is accepted as the moral ideal. However, certain people in particular circumstances (i.e., those born into warrior castes or called to be police officers) cannot follow the ideal, nor are they expected to. They can, however, carry out their calling while practicing as little violence as necessary to meet the needs of their communities. Perhaps a future lifetime will provide them with the luxury of a life of nonviolence. This stands in contrast to the Western model, where the violence of those called to such livelihoods must be shown to be morally acceptable (as in just war theory), or even praiseworthy, and thus not a necessary evil. This distinction will play an important role in understanding the next chapters, as we consider the moral question of whether or not nonviolence is truly praiseworthy.

PART TWO

Nonviolent Possibilities

There are many causes I would die for.
There is not a single cause I would kill for.

—Mohandas Gandhi

Even war is a good exchange for a miserable peace.

—Tacitus

"Pacifism? Really?"

Many years ago, I attended a Quaker high school. The Society of Friends, as I discovered, is one of the traditions within Christianity with a long and sincere commitment to pacifism. As a typical red-blooded American teenager, I regarded this ethical conviction as naïve. From both a religious and practical perspective, my reaction to it was usually to roll my eyes. "Really? It was wrong to fight for American independence, against slavery, against the Nazis?"

To be sure, there were plenty of slogans for nonviolence that did little to persuade me. I reacted with typical sophomoric arrogance:

"There are causes worth dying for, but none worth killing for." I think the soldiers who liberated Dachau and Buchenwald would disagree.

"Resist all injustices nonviolently!" So says the best friend a tyrant ever had?

"War creates peace, like hate creates love." Cute cliché, but have you ever taken a history class?

Trite arguments such as these are, of course, still around. I still encounter overreactions to violence from time to time that do little to persuade me to adopt nonviolence as a guiding ethic. In 2016, an article in *USA Today* reported on a little girl who was sent home from school with a note telling her parents to find her a new lunchbox. The offending image she had dared to take to school: Wonder Woman. The school explained, "The dress code we have established requests that the children not bring violent images into the building in any fashion . . . We have defined 'violent characters' as those who solve problems using violence. Superheroes . . . fall into that category."[4] So would every US president, for that matter.

Today, I am a little older, wiser, and less quick to judgment than I was in high school. I remain unconvinced by those who oppose all violence, but I have gained an appreciation for the perspective of many of them. A fair and open-minded examination of the ethics of nonviolence is like studying another religion. I may not convert, but understanding what others believe—their deepest convictions—is always of tremendous value. At the same time, I am likely to find insights of significant worth, and maybe even some inspiration.

Pacifism and Nonviolence

It may appear that I am using these words interchangeably throughout this chapter, but that is not quite the case. Traditionally, pacifism has been associated with certain western ethics that oppose direct violence to other human beings. "Nonviolence," on the other hand, is a broader objection to the use of violence, which may include the consumption of meat or indirect support of the violent actions of others.

There is no single expression of either of these ethics. Some pacifists accept a certain level of non-lethal violence in certain circumstances, while others do not. Among those practicing the ethics of nonviolence, this may or may not include vegetarianism. There are some who even wear a cloth mask over their mouths, so as to avoid accidentally inhaling small airborne insects. It can sometimes include opposition to certain vocations that advance violence, like working at Lockheed Martin to help build military aircraft. While "nonviolence" often functions as the umbrella term, there is a multiplicity of pacifisms and practices of nonviolence.

4. Goldberg, "Softheaded Moralizing at School."

Types of Pacifism

Pacifism has no singular expression. Douglas P. Lackey has written a helpful article on the subject, where he differentiates four types:

1. Opposition to all killing.

2. Opposition to all violence.

3. Opposition to all personal violence (but not all state violence).

4. Opposition to all state violence (but not all personal violence).[5]

Thus, it is important to be aware of what type of "pacifism" any individual is advocating when considering its ethical merits. Throughout this book, we will engage various expressions of these four types.[6]

Lackey also briefly treats the subject of the personal pacifist. This is the individual who states that she personally will not engage in violence or killing, but does not believe it is wrong for others to do so. Lackey derisively waves away this idea, claiming that it does not constitute a genuine moral code. For Lackey, and many others in the West,[7] an ethic that is not universal is not valid. "If pacifism is to be a moral theory, it must be prescribed for all or prescribed for none."[8]

I believe this critique of individual pacifism is seriously flawed. Lackey dismisses this individual ethic as just sloppy relativism, but that is not necessarily the case. Our religious and cultural traditions are full of examples of men and women who chose (or felt called to) a different ethical code without denigrating what others followed. The Hebrew Bible/Old Testament describes the Nazirites, like Samson, who were set aside within society. They let their hair grow long, visited gravesites, and vowed to avoid alcohol. In following this lifestyle, it was never suggested that imbibing, haircuts, and avoiding contact with the dead were immoral. Likewise, within the Christian monastic tradition, we find men and women taking an oath to live by an ethic of poverty, chastity, and obedience. This is not understood to imply that the majority who marry and accumulate property are acting immorally. In Asia, this kind of aspirational individual ethic has played a tremendous role in eastern religions, among Hindu sadhus and Buddhist monks. In fact,

5. Lackey, "Pacifism," 7–21.

6. To be certain, there are other "types" of pacifism, such as "conditional-utilitarian" and "conditional-deontological," as well as proposals for new categories, like "proportionality-based" and "epistemic-based" pacifisms, as in Bazargan, "Varieties of Contingent Pacifism in War."

7. Lee, *Ethics and War*, 22.

8. Lackey, "Pacifism," 8.

I believe that the most compelling type of pacifistic ethic is this individualistic commitment, as I shall argue below.

There are also those who think of themselves as pacifists because they reject war and violence in most cases, even if they are not universally opposed to it. These people believe that fighting should only be as a "last resort," but they do not rule it out completely. This position is sometimes referred to as "contingent pacifism," "pacific-ism," or we may simply speak of them as "doves." However, their position is essentially the same as those who fall into the "just war" camp: war is unfortunate and requires a strong justification, but it is not an absolute wrong. The distinction is simply that they view conditions differently when considering whether killing is justified. Therefore, we should reserve the word "pacifist" for those who universally condemn killing, or violence, as unacceptable—at least for themselves.

In the remainder of this section, we will consider the various ethics of nonviolence, first in the West and then in the East. While I will argue that absolute nonviolence as a universal moral code is an untenable ethic, I do hope that the reader comes to share some of my appreciation for what pacifists and others committed to nonviolence bring to the table. An honest engagement with these traditions brings considerable clarity and critical insight into the discussion of the ethics of violence.

CHAPTER 3

Nonviolence in the West

I am not only a pacifist but a militant pacifist. I am willing to fight for peace. Nothing will end war unless the people themselves refuse to go to war.

—ALBERT EINSTEIN

O f the three major western religious traditions, Christianity is the one with the longest and most significant history of pacifism. With apologies to Muslim and Jewish pacifists, this section will only consider Christian pacifism, as it is this group who has actively debated this moral question for nearly two millennia. Furthermore, many of the Muslim and Jewish pacifist arguments are expressed within the Christian dialogue as well. With regard to secular pacifists, who typically rely on utilitarian arguments, we will consider their perspectives later in this chapter.

The Hebrew Bible/Old Testament

Judaism does not have a significant tradition of pacifism, although recent centuries have seen individual Jewish pacifists who argue for the moral uprightness of nonviolence. The Hebrew Scriptures, what Christians call the Old Testament, contain a great amount of law and history in which violence is practiced, condoned, and even commanded in certain circumstances. In this respect, ancient Israel was no different than nearly every other nation on earth.

There is one place, however, where God issues a command that appears to many as a call for nonviolence. The fifth commandment (or sixth, depending on how you number them) given to Moses is often translated as "thou shalt not kill." This divine command is often cited to argue that killing another human being is wrong. However, such an interpretation is clearly not what was intended or understood in ancient Israel. The word that was used is *ratzach*, which means "murder." It is only the killing of an innocent that is condemned here. This commandment has nothing to do with self-defense, war, or capital punishment.[1]

Jesus of Nazareth

According to some, the origin of the Christian ethic of nonviolence is found in Jesus of Nazareth. It is he who Christians regard as the Son of God, the incarnation of the second person of the Trinity. In traditional Christianity, his word and example are absolute—literally the Word of God. For Christians, Jesus' moral instruction constitutes divine command ethics.

A significant number of Christians over the centuries have read the Gospels of Jesus Christ and concluded that he taught an ethic of nonviolence. There is compelling material in those texts that can lead people, like renowned theologian Stanley Hauerwas, to the conclusion that "Christians cannot seek justice from the barrel of a gun."[2] To some, it appears so obvious to be beyond dispute. Pacifist philosopher Robert W. Brimlow boldly asserts, "I think it is simply so clear that the gospel includes violence and killing on the list of actions that Christians may not perform that I honestly do not know what more could be added."[3]

As it turns out, they are wrong.

There are certainly plenty of places in the Gospels where Jesus appears to advocate an ethic of nonviolence: "turn the other cheek"; "put away your sword"; "my kingdom is not of this world." His personal example, likewise, can be understood as a compelling argument for nonviolence. Though innocent of any wrongdoing, he did not oppose the Jewish Council or Romans; but was "like a sheep who before his shearers is silent, so he did not open his mouth." Despite having both the authority and resources to overthrow worldly powers, he quite explicitly rejected this course of action.

1. The word for general killing in Hebrew is *harag*. In the Septuagint, the authoritative Greek translation of the Hebrew scriptures, *ratzach* is translated as *phoneuseis*, which also carries the meaning of "murder" in English.

2. Hauerwas, *Peaceable Kingdom*, 104.

3. Brimlow, *What About Hitler*, 31.

However, if we undertake a more careful reading of these texts, coupled with some context, the argument that Jesus taught an ethic of nonviolence falls apart.

To begin with, we must remember that Jesus was Jewish. For millennia, the Israelites had engaged in war when commanded to by God. They had a military, they practiced capital punishment, and they defended themselves with arms against outlaws and enemies. This was his culture, his religion, his absolute moral framework. If Jesus was going to overturn all of that, he would need to be pretty explicit about it. The Messiah who did not come to abolish the law, but to fulfill it, never demanded that his followers forsake all violence. It is true that he changed a few specific things. He taught that one can lust or murder within one's heart and still be guilty of sin. He relaxed certain legal absolutes—e.g., healing on the Sabbath. However, no one can point to a teaching of Jesus that introduces something as radical (especially in that time and place) as universal nonviolence.

There are those who suggest that the Old Testament featured a more legalistic and less forgiving God, when compared to Jesus in the New Testament. This is highly problematic. John Yoder (1927–1997), the famous Christian pacifist, tried this argument. "The Jews were then living in the age of law and judgment; while we dwell in the dispensation of grace and mercy!"[4] Yoder appears confused about the Christian distinction between how God deals with repentant sinners and how governments should deal with them. It is true that "law and judgment" were established for the nation of Israel; Jesus spoke of the "grace and mercy" that come from God to the repentant believer. However, this is apples and oranges. It is silly to suggest that Jesus' message of grace and mercy means that citizens of a nation are no longer subject to laws and judgment. Doing so would mean that no one could even be fined or imprisoned!

Suggesting a God of justice in the Old Testament, as compared to a God of love and mercy in the New Testament, creates other problems. This kind of theology smacks of Marcionism, the heresy of the third century that taught that the God of the Old Testament was inferior to the God and Father of Jesus found in the New Testament. Christians have rejected this teaching ever since, and many would rightly point out that it can carry an anti-Jewish undertone that does not square well with Christian scriptures or theology.

But didn't Jesus teach that we should love our neighbors as ourselves, and treat others as we wish to be treated? He did, of course. However, that certainly does not mean that you or I may never use violence. As Brimlow

---

4. Yoder, *What Would You Do*, 51. Brimlow argues the same thing, announcing that "Jesus overturns . . . mandatory sentencing guidelines . . . clearly indicating that what stood before as justifications no longer stand" (*What About Hitler*, 31).

argues, "There is no way I can read [Scripture] and consider that Jesus meant to teach us; 'Form a deep abiding love for the one who strikes you, and then knock his teeth out in response to his aggression.'"[5] This is, of course, a straw-man argument. Moreover, this sappy ethic of love has some obvious problems. A universal ethic of love requires me to love the aggressor, but also all of his potential victims. Failing to stop a violent criminal—through whatever means are deemed legal by the state—is a failure to love my neighbor.

If I witness a man snatch an elderly lady's purse and take off running down the sidewalk, would I be loving my neighbor(s) if I just let him go? If I chased him down and tackled him, I would be acting violently. (Being tackled on cement while at a full sprint can really hurt!) However, restoring the woman's property is certainly in accordance with love. Deterring the purse snatcher—and other potential purse snatchers—from future criminal activities is also in accordance with love. If I catch him, and then proceed to beat his head into the sidewalk for thirty seconds, then yes, that would not be loving. That would be a violation of the law, and clearly not in the service of my community.

The Golden Rule ("Do unto others as you would have them do unto you") does not preclude violence or punishment. It is absurd to ask, "Would you want someone to tackle you if you had stolen an old lady's purse?" Of course not! And I would not want to be thrown in jail if I killed someone, but no one is advocating for closing down all prisons. Clearly that is not what Jesus meant. Such an application of the Golden Rule is obviously flawed. So, if we return to Brimlow's quaint notion that love means I can never punch anyone in the face, we see that it is an inadequate ethic. In the words of Reinhold Niebuhr (1892–1971), regarded by many as the greatest American theologian of the twentieth century, "It is impossible to construct a social ethic out of the ideal of love in its pure form."[6] Jesus' radical call for love—even of one's enemies—is not a call to universal pacifism.

Jesus did say, however, that we should turn the other cheek if struck in the face. This ethical teaching, found in the Sermon on the Mount (Matt 5:39), is a favorite of many people. It is also one of mine. However, it does not teach what many people believe. It is very important to note that when Jesus tells his disciples how to respond to those who "strike" them, he is not describing a self-defense situation. The word he uses in Greek is *hrapizo*, which means a strike with an open hand. Jesus is describing a situation in which someone slaps you, not where someone swings a tire-iron at your

5. Brimlow, *What About Hitler*, 31.

6. Niebuhr, *Interpretation of Christian Ethics*, 91.

head. A slap is typically an assault on a person's dignity, not an attempt to knock you out and steal your shekels. The ethic of Jesus is that when your dignity is on the line, do not escalate the violence. Imagine how much needless violence could be avoided if we followed this teaching! This is an ethic worth sharing and cultivating within ourselves. It is not, however, a call to universal nonviolence.

Recall that Jesus also told his foremost disciple Peter to put away his sword when he cut off Malchus's ear in the Garden of Gethsemane (John 18:11). This quote, again, might appear to be a call for pacifism, but one must ask, "What is Peter doing with a sword in the first place?" If Jesus had been teaching a new ethic of absolute nonviolence, why did Peter and at least one other disciple (Luke 22:38) have them under their cloaks? While one might suggest that they did not truly understand Jesus' message (which was often the case), pay attention to Jesus' words. He did not tell Peter to throw away his sword, or beat it into a plowshare, but to put it back in its sheath (*thēkē*). Earlier, when he was told that the disciples had two swords, he replied, "That is enough." It would appear that Jesus knew his disciples were packing weapons, presumably for self-defense, and had no problem with it. It was not until they thought about fighting against the Jewish authorities, however, that Jesus stepped in to curb their enthusiasm.[7]

We might also add that Jesus' encounters with military personnel do not produce any condemnation of their profession. The centurion, whose servant Jesus heals, is commended for having faith greater than anyone in Israel (Matt 8:10). Likewise, John the Baptist—a man who never refrained from moral chastisement—told the soldiers what was expected of them: "Don't extort money and don't accuse people falsely—be content with your pay" (Luke 3:14). Some may argue that, while Jesus and John the Baptist never condemned the occupations of those in the military, they never explicitly condoned their profession either. However, if we are to make an "argument from silence," we must assume the social norms in the narrative. The Gospel accounts are set in a social context that permitted the use of violence in the service of law and order.

It is also true that Jesus caused quite a scene at the temple, even making a whip out of cords (John 2:15). In 2014, I wrote a short article arguing that

---

7. There are some who contend that Peter was carrying a "knife," not a "sword," as the word *machaira* may be translated. However, as Palmer notes, the word is often used throughout the New Testatment to refer to a sword. It is never used to refer to what is clearly a "knife," as detailed in *Christian Pacifism and Just War Theory*, 32–34. Moreover, the noun *machē* is translated as "battle," and the verb *machesthai* is "to fight." There is no good reason to believe that Peter pulled out anything other than a small sword which would have been designed and carried for use as a weapon.

this constituted violent behavior on his part, as he was running everyone out of the temple courtyard. That argument, unfortunately, does not stand up to scrutiny. The Greek is not clear whether he used the whip on people and animals, or just animals. Thus, we cannot say that Jesus' behavior in the temple constituted violence. It is ambiguous. A suggestion from a friend, however, does intrigue me: one must wonder why the money-changers did not do more to stop the antics of Jesus, unless his disciples were at his back, perhaps with their hands on the hilts of a couple of swords. This, of course, is pure speculation.

On the basis of the Gospels, we must acknowledge that Jesus himself lived a nonviolent life. He spoke out against pride and greed. He praised those who are peacemakers. He did not resist those who arrested and killed him. However, he appeared to take certain realities of the world for granted, such as the need for police, a military, and carrying weapons for self-defense. Nowhere can one find him advocating a break with the laws and customs of Israel in favor of a new absolute ethic of nonviolence or pacifism.

Certainly what Jesus desired when he blessed the peacemakers was the establishing of *shalom*. This Hebrew word, which attempts to capture the ideals of peace, unity, and harmony—both between God and human beings, and also between human beings themselves—is at the heart of Jesus' ethic. As discussed in the introduction to this book, *shalom* and *salaam* convey more than the absence of fighting. Contrary to Cicero, an unjust peace is not always better than a just war. Jesus' blessing of the peacemakers was not a new law that the disciples allow the world to run roughshod over them and others, but to do what is necessary to move us in the direction of the ideal of *shalom* or *salaam*.

It is true that Christians are called upon to adhere to the example of Jesus, take up their crosses, and follow him. While Jesus is the moral example *par excellence*, it does not follow that believers are to imitate everything that he did. Jesus offered no defense at his trial. Are Christians obliged to forego defense attorneys? Jesus was celibate. Few Christians are called to an imitation of that. Jesus was an unemployed, homeless, itinerant preacher. Must all Christians follow suit? Jesus had his own particular mission, one which required him to live and act in ways that have never been understood as requirements for all of his followers. The command to follow Jesus is fulfilled in the imitation of his virtues, not the particulars of his life and calling. The desire for *shalom/salaam* is to be held in common, but the methods to achieve that will necessarily vary.

To sum up, we do not find any divine command of nonviolence in the Gospel accounts of Jesus' life. If Christians are to be pacifist, they must do so on the basis of other moral argumentation. Perhaps it is the prudent thing to do, or the virtuous thing, but there is no basis for the claim that an absolute call to pacifism has its foundation in the moral teachings of Jesus. The call to be peacemakers, however, is a moral imperative and divine command. Unfortunately, in this twisted world, those who are ready and able to fight are often greater peacekeepers than those unable or unwilling to do so. The sad lesson of Rwanda and its impotent United Nations peacekeepers only reinforces this truth.

The Early Church

It is often argued that Christians in the first few centuries after Christ were pacifists up until the time of Constantine (c. 272–337 AD). This is not exactly true. It is not false, either, but it is a significant oversimplification of a more complex reality in the early church. As political theologian Oliver O'Donovan explains, to speak of early church "pacifists" does not really make sense, given the historical context, "since the question of military service was not disentangled from the general question of involvement with a hostile pagan government."[8]

First, we must recognize that Christianity in the first few centuries was a tremendously diverse religion. There were polytheists (Marcionites and certain gnostics), anti-Trinitarians (Montanists and other gnostics), those who denied Jesus' humanity (Docetists), those who denied his divinity (Arians), and a host of others. Any statement about what early Christians believed must be viewed with suspicion.

To be sure, there were significant early church fathers who spoke out against serving in the military, or any kind of violence. Clement of Alexandria (c. 150–c. 215 AD), Tertullian (c. 155–c. 240 AD), and Origen (184/185–253/254 AD) are probably the three best-known and most influential in these early centuries. Additionally, there were early Christians who were martyred because they refused to serve in the military. These men of faith demonstrated the sincerity of their ethical convictions, and ultimately paid for this decision with their lives.

However, the religious objections from these particular Christians must be placed in their proper context. For example, Clement taught that Christianity, in its ideal form, is pacifistic. His view was comparable to what we find among Roman Catholics today. The ideal is a world in which there is no war, no violence. However, given our fallen world, serving honorably in the military is an option that can be pursued without risk to one's soul. There are those who strive to live by the ideal, and there are others who may

8. O'Donovan, *Just War Revisited*, 11.

live according to a more modest moral standard. James Turner Johnson explains, "As a result, his attitude toward military service for Christians was a foreshadowing of the distinction that later emerged, in both East and West, allowing military service for Christian laity but forbidding it to monks and clergy."[9]

Tertullian, one of the most profound of the Latin church fathers, clearly rejected the possibility that a Christian could serve as a soldier. He was definitely a pacifist. Nevertheless, his view on soldiering did not spring from an absolute ethic of nonviolence, but a rejection of the world. Tertullian also rejected the proposition that a Christian could be a student or teacher, as the schools taught Greek and Roman literature which was essentially pagan. He spoke out against serving in the Roman civil service. He called for a complete rejection of the world, as he raised the following rhetorical question: "What has Athens to do with Jerusalem?"

Tertullian's extreme moral rigor was an extension of earlier Christian rejections of this world while waiting for the return of Christ. Again, Turner puts it succinctly:

> The rejection of military service by first-century Christians was part of a broader phenomenon of separation from the life of "the world" that also extended to include a preference for celibacy and virginity over marriage and rejection of individual ownership of property. They sought to separate themselves in this way because they believed the end of the world was at hand and were seeking to prepare themselves for the life of the new age to come.[10]

It is also worth pointing out that Tertullian's moral extremism eventually led him to join the heretical group known as the Montanists, who were condemned by the Catholic church.

The third church father was Origen, a man of strong passion and convictions. As a boy, his mother had to hide his clothes at one point to keep him from going outside and seeking martyrdom during a particular persecution, the one that took his father's life. Later, we are told that he took a literal reading of Jesus' advice in Matthew 5:30 ("If your hand causes you to sin, cut it off") and castrated himself.[11] While we have extensive writings from Origen, he speaks only briefly of his opposition to war. In these writings, however, he makes it clear that he rejected military service for

9. Johnson, *Quest for Peace*, 21.

10. Johnson, *Ethics and the Use of Force*, 16.

11. Jesus had taught that it is better for you to lose a single part of your body than for your entire body to go to hell.

Christians. His justification appears to be a genuine commitment to non-violence and his conviction that Christians must do what they can to foster peace. For Origen, this meant refusal to serve in the military.

While there were Christians who staunchly opposed careers in the army for various reasons, there was still a considerable number of Christians who disagreed. Even before Constantine, the number of Christians serving Rome with arms increased—sometimes reaching sufficient numbers to prompt a purge of them by pagan officers who viewed them with suspicion. The *Legio Fulminata* (the "Thundering Legion") was a Roman military unit that possessed a particularly large number of believers. By the beginning of the fourth century, there may have been tens of thousands of Christians in the Roman army.[12]

The early church, then, was a highly diverse religious body where Christians held a number of different attitudes regarding military service for a variety of reasons. There was no single or dominant position on the subject, as is still the case today. While the church fathers provide us with insight regarding this ethical issue, and should be valued because of it, they do not provide us with the view of early Christians on the subject because there was none.[13]

The Radical Reformation

The next period of church history in which one finds a significant number of pacifists does not arrive until the sixteenth century. The period known as the Reformation is generally recognized to have begun in 1517, when Martin Luther (1483–1546) nailed his ninety-five theses to the church door in Wittenberg. Thereafter, figures like Luther, Ulrich Zwingli (1484–1531), and John Calvin (1509–1564) challenged the Roman Catholic tradition they had received, eventually creating Protestants. On the issue of war and violence, these reformers held the same basic position as the Roman Catholics. However, they did offer a few changes when they themselves were attacked by forces loyal to the Pope. They explicitly accepted the idea of a just war, the right to personal self-defense in particular circumstances, and they rejected pacifism. Zwingli actually died in combat, battleaxe in hand, fighting the Catholics in Switzerland.

As these men helped usher in the period known as the Reformation, there were others who decided that the reformers were not taking things

12. Johnson, *Quest for Peace*, 44.

13. This overview is necessarily brief, but interested readers can find the topic treated with much greater depth in Johnson's excellent book, *The Quest for Peace*.

far enough. Groups like the Anabaptists (so named because they believed in re-baptizing Christians who had first been baptized as infants) became part of the Radical Reformation. Many of these Anabaptists were pacifists, though not all of them. Some, like Thomas Müntzer (c. 1489–1525), were in fact quite violent!

The Church of the Brethren, Hutterites, and Mennonites were part of this movement and explicitly taught pacifism. Later, these were joined by the Amish (who split from the Mennonites). Other pacifist groups would also develop later, like the Religious Society of Friends (better known as the Quakers). These traditions believed pacifism to be an essential aspect of Jesus' message in the Gospels, not a personal preference. They did not consider nonviolence a calling for the spiritual elite, like Clement did earlier. Rather, it was required of all believers. While the Amish have coupled their nonviolence with a rejection of "the world," like Tertullian, other traditions have been actively involved in social and political movements since their inception.

All of these groups faced persecution in their early years. Thousands were martyred—killed for their faith by both Protestants and Catholics. While some of the animosity they faced was due to other theological issues, like the rejection of infant baptism, their pacifism was not insignificant. Today, it is easy to ask why anyone would get so mad at a pacifist. One may regard them as naïve, or poor interpreters of Scripture, but how angry can you get at a person who won't fight?

These new religious movements were seen as a direct threat to the stability of their communities. A prince who oversees a small and contested area of land would not be too keen on upstart religious leaders telling his people that Jesus forbids them from serving in the military or defending their land through force of arms. Even a noble ruler would recognize this as a danger to his people and to himself, a threat to peace. How much more a tyrant who was bent on recruiting a military for more nefarious purposes? It may appear ironic at first, but it does follow that the preaching of pacifism can sometimes lead to less peace, not more.

If a nation is large and powerful enough in comparison to its neighbors, then the existence of pacifists among their people may be of little concern. This may account for the increasing tolerance of conscientious objectors in the history of the United States. Early on, refusal of military service resulted in imprisonment or fines. For almost a century, however, sincere opposition to war is sufficient to obtain conscientious objector status.

Today, we still find religious traditions within Christianity that are historically pacifistic. This does not mean, of course, that every member of these denominations is a pacifist. (President Richard Nixon was a Quaker.)

At the same time, there are members of other denominations and western religions that are not part of this tradition—groups that may explicitly support the use of violence as divinely sanctioned—who personally choose to embrace pacifism (e.g., Martin Niemoller—Lutheranism; Martin Buber—Judaism; Nafez Assaily—Islam).

Summary of Christian Nonviolence

What shall we say, then, about Christianity and nonviolence? It is clear that the Old Testament did not teach an ethic of nonviolence. While we all want to live in a world where we can beat our swords into plowshares, our world does not currently allow for that, nor did the world of the Israelites. The use of violence against their enemies was, at times, even sanctioned by the God of the Israelites.

Jesus of Nazareth was first and foremost a Jew. He did not perceive his life and ministry as the leader of a worldly kingdom, but a spiritual one. As such, he deliberately chose to live a life of nonviolence. However, his interactions with the disciples and others clearly convey that he was not establishing some new ethic of universal nonviolence. There is no divine command.

The subsequent history of Christianity has seen great diversity of thought and theology. While an ethic of nonviolence has always been present, the vast majority of Christians have condoned the use of arms by certain people and in certain circumstances. Nothing in scripture, including the very words of Jesus, can be considered a moral imperative to nonviolence. Moreover, emulating the virtues of Jesus does not demand pacifism. Christians are not called to imitate every action of Jesus. While the virtue of being a peacemaker (*pacifici* in Latin) may be divinely mandated, there is no single model for such a person. We find lovers of peace represented among anti-war protestors, United Nations peacekeepers, and state troopers who all want nothing but peace and concord in their communities.

Utilitarian Nonviolence

A Christian call for an ethic of nonviolence cannot be based on divine command, but it may find its support in utilitarian reasoning. To do so, it must clearly express how this moral commitment will achieve greater human happiness and thriving.

Arguing that a universal commitment to nonviolence achieves the greatest good for the greatest number is a hard sell. In 2015, international attention turned to the story of prospective terrorist Ayoub El-Khazzani, who was intent on slaughtering a large number of people aboard a French train. Fortunately, he failed. A French humanities professor, of all people, managed to strip him of the AK-47 he was wielding before being shot by El-Khazzani's secondary weapon, a pistol. At that point, a trio of Americans, two of whom served in the military, stormed down the aisle of the car and relieved the man of his handgun. El-Khazzani then pulled a tertiary weapon, a box-cutter, and sliced up one of the Americans. He was eventually pummeled and choked into submission. While the situation did not necessitate the killing of El-Khazzani, it is not difficult to imagine how it might have required lethal force if things had played out a little differently. All things considered, it is hard to script a better response to this despicable attempt at mass murder. It is even harder to argue that the passengers on that French train would have been better off if their railcar had been full of pacifists.

People often present hypothetical scenarios similar to this one. They want to make the point that there are times when violence, even deadly violence, serves the common good. Should we not have fought against the Nazis? Were the passengers on United Airlines Flight 93 wrong to assault the 9/11 hijackers? What if someone is going to kill your family and you have access to a gun? To their credit, many pacifists have been willing to respond to such questions. John H. Yoder even wrote a book about it, entitled *What Would You Do?*[14]

Often, Christian pacifist arguments to these hard questions fall back on the claim that God would not allow someone to be put in a situation where violence was the only possible solution. We have already seen that western religions cannot point to a divine command that demands universal nonviolence. Similarly, the claim that God will provide a "way of escape," so that violence is not necessary, rests on belief in some alleged guarantee that is not scriptural.[15] God never promised such a thing in the Bible. The only argument left is utilitarian, the possibility that individuals who choose a complete rejection of violence will achieve a greater happiness for human beings.

As discussed in chapter 1, the fundamental challenge of utilitarian ethics is that one never knows the effects of one's actions. The best of intentions sometimes result in disastrous consequences. Giving money to a beggar on the street does not always result in the good we imagine. Making the

14. See also Brimlow, *What About Hitler.*

15. E.g., Yoder, *What Would You Do,* 34. St. Paul's promise that God will not allow one to be tested beyond what he can bear (1 Cor 10:13) does not apply here, as it speaks of a way to avoid sin. Yoder has failed to make the case that violence is always a sin.

argument that violence will improve a situation is impossible when we do not know what will ultimately happen.

Consider the example of Dietrich Bonhoeffer (1906–1945), one of my personal heroes. A German Lutheran pastor and theologian during the Third Reich, Bonhoeffer was deeply committed to peace. He was a great admirer of Gandhi, and had made plans to visit him in India after the war. However, he also knew that the violence of war is not something so qualitatively different than what can take place during "peace." He wrote:

> It is not war that first brings death, not war that first invents the pains and torments of human bodies and souls, not war that first unleashes lies, injustice, and violence. It is not war that first makes our existence so utterly precarious and renders human beings powerless, forcing them to watch their desires and plans being thwarted and destroyed by more "exalted powers." But war makes all of this, which existed already apart from it and before it, vast and unavoidable to us who would gladly prefer to overlook it all.[16]

Despite the horrors of war, Bonhoeffer became convinced that Hitler needed to be stopped; he felt a moral obligation to act, even if it meant supporting assassination. He famously explained to his sister-in-law, "If I see a madman driving a car into a group of innocent bystanders, then I can't, as a Christian, simply wait for the catastrophe and then comfort the wounded and bury the dead. I must try to wrestle the steering wheel out of the hands of the driver." It is not enough to provide care to the victims; one must "jam a spoke in the wheel itself." Bonhoeffer eventually became a co-conspirator in an attempt to assassinate Hitler.

Although they failed, we may ask what would have happened had they succeeded. The eventual suicide of Hitler brought the war to an end, allowed an unconditional surrender, and permitted a fundamental break with Germany's Nazi identity. This may have been impossible if the earlier assassination attempt by Bonhoeffer's colleagues had succeeded. Hitler would have been martyred, and others would have taken control who might have kept fighting more effectively or negotiated a conditional surrender. In hindsight, Bonhoeffer's act of violence could well have made the world a much worse place.

This inability to see the future, to know the consequences of our actions, is often cited by pacifists as a reason to eschew violence. An act of violence often makes things even worse. Yoder correctly points out, "The

---

16. As in Metaxas, *Bonhoeffer*, 373.

outcome of any kind of combat is unpredictable."[17] Famed pacifist Leo Tolstoy (1828–1910) took things a step further when he pointed out that, in making the decision to engage in violence, the only outcome you can be sure of is that you will cause harm through violence. Even if a criminal is threatening a child, should a person "decide to kill the criminal in order to defend the child? By killing the former he kills for certain; whereas he cannot know positively whether the criminal would have killed the child or not."[18]

While it is true that we do not know the consequences of our actions, and that an act of perceived "just violence" may result in greater suffering than the commitment to peace, it is a logical error to conclude that we should therefore never engage in violence. Utilitarians must analyze the anticipated costs and benefits of their behaviors. While we cannot know with absolute certainty the consequences of our actions, we can engage in critical thinking to try to achieve the best for our world. We will not get it right 100 percent of the time, and so the fact that we make mistakes should drive us to greater care in our decision-making, not inaction. Waiting for absolute certainty of anything leads only to paralysis. It would make no sense to say that I should never give to charity because sometimes charities are ineffective. Likewise, it is absurd to say that I should never engage in violence because sometimes violence makes things worse. This observation should lead to greater care in our ethical decision-making, especially with regard to violence, but not the inability to act because of the possibility of unforeseen consequences.

One thing should be clear: unwillingness to ever engage in violence carries plenty of scary potential consequences of its own. As Rory Miller and Lawrence Kane present in their excellent book *Scaling Force*, "Most bad guys resort to violence expecting to have no bad consequences, and they are usually right. Unless someone steps in (and is willing to risk all that comes on the line in a violent encounter), most low-level violence is rewarded, not punished. Civilians can, and often do, look the other way."[19]

While Tolstoy is right that engaging in violence to achieve something good only guarantees violence, not necessarily the intended outcome, Miller and Kane make an equally important point. When a group of people categorically refuse even to consider the possibility of violence, criminals face fewer negative consequences. They are then more likely to engage in

17. Yoder, *What Would You Do*, 15.

18. Yoder, *What Would You Do*, 36.

19. Miller and Kane, *Scaling Force*, 63.

criminal behavior. Hence, the old saying, "Make yourselves sheep, and the wolves will eat you."[20]

What is necessary is the prudence and wisdom to consider whether an act of violence has a high likelihood of resulting in a greater good. For those eager to use violence in order to achieve good, a habit of restraint is probably a wise investment. My mother always said, "Discretion is the better part of valor." At the same time, those inclined to think that pacifism and diplomacy can always win the day must remember that they too hold an unhealthy bias. For academics in our ivory towers, who enjoy lives of study and collegiality in safe environments, we must remember that our perception of the harsh realities of the world is usually skewed. Not everyone in the world is as civil and diplomatic as a room full of college professors. Reinhold Niebuhr speaks of such a privileged member of society. "He sees moral forces working efficaciously within the confines of his group, and erroneously imagines that they can be extended until they resolve all group conflict."[21] He goes on to say, "If a season of violence can establish a just social system and can create the possibilities of its preservation, there is no purely ethical ground upon which violence and revolution can be ruled out."[22]

From the perspective of act-utilitarianism, if a thoughtful, well-informed, critical analysis of a situation leads one to the conclusion that a greater good is served through a use of violence, then a categorical rejection of such an act is not morally defensible. For the rule-utilitarian, we may add that when people of moral conscience categorically refuse to engage in violence—thinking it will do more good than harm in the long run—they forget that promising to never use violence only emboldens and encourages those with the inclination to victimize others.

From a utilitarian perspective, however, I do not believe that pacifism is worthless. I am happy that there are pacifists, even if I disagree with them. While I believe they fail to make the case that violence never makes the world a better place (an act-utilitarian perspective), or that a greater good is served when motivated individuals eschew all violence (a rule-utilitarian perspective), I am still appreciative that they are among us. I believe their presence is conducive to human thriving and happiness, for they demand that the rest of us provide the strongest arguments to justify acts of violence.

---

20. Mentioned by Benjamin Franklin in a letter to his sister, Jane Mecom, written on November 1, 1773.

21. Niebuhr, *Moral Man and Immoral Society*, 179.

22. Niebuhr, *Moral Man and Immoral Society*, 179.

They challenge us to reconsider our inclinations toward fighting and are an important counterweight to human nature's penchant for violence.

Stanley Hauerwas, the pacifist theologian discussed above, has made arguments for pacifism that fail to persuade this author of the moral superiority of that ethic. However, I appreciate his constant reminders that a willingness to engage in violence often leads to unnecessary violence. In *The Peaceable Kingdom*, he writes, "[W]e fear the lack of control a commitment to peace would entail. As a result the more we seek to bring 'under our control,' the more violent we have to become to protect what we have. And the more violent we allow ourselves to become, the more vulnerable we are to challenges."[23]

Hauerwas's argument has led me to a bit of self-reflection. When I first began studying martial arts in college, I was attracted by the idea of being able to defend myself. As time went by, I wanted to learn more about the ways of violence, to be able to respond to increasingly dangerous situations. I learned quite a bit about dishing out some substantial physical violence, just in case it was ever needed. By the time I earned my brown belt, I had some legitimate skill. I also had the habit of looking around at all the potential threats that could come my way, and how I could respond to them violently. (For those not familiar with karate and similar arts, this is what we call "brown belt syndrome.") It would take a long time to reprogram myself to think about how best to respond to situations nonviolently, regardless of my ability to defend myself physically.

Hauerwas continues to discuss how a willingness to solve problems with violence can circumvent our ability to think imaginatively of alternatives to violence. "[W]hen violence is justified in principle as a necessary strategy for securing justice, it stills the imaginative search for nonviolent ways of resistance to justice."[24] If I believe I am morally justified in coming to the aid of someone getting beaten up by violently engaging the attacker, I am much more likely to do so. I may not consider the plethora of nonviolent options to achieve the same end.

There is a humorous video on the internet showing three guys who individually put themselves in dangerous situations where a fistfight with a stranger is about to break out. However, at the moment when the fur is about to fly, the one fellow pulls his pants and underpants completely down. Invariably, the other guy decides he doesn't want to fight with a half-naked man and runs off. Violence avoided! (Admittedly, the three guys in the video

---

23. Hauerwas, *Peaceable Kingdom*, 49.

24. Hauerwas, *Peaceable Kingdom*, 114.

first stirred up the confrontation, but their way of stopping the violence, which was on the cusp of happening, was intriguing.)

Such a strategy will obviously not work in all situations, but it does provide an example of how creative thinking can very often find nonviolent answers when it is committed to do so. Pacifists like Hauerwas do us a service when they remind us of this fact.

Pacifists also provide us with the service of pointing out that people who believe violence is sometimes justified can become very good at justifying *any* violence. With regard to advocates of just war theory, Brimlow argues, "They seem able to justify almost all wars rather than to provide a means to limit the number of wars that would be considered just."[25] This is surely an overstatement, but he is certainly right that we humans are very good at justifying our actions—both to ourselves and to others. If there is never an allowance for violence, the argument goes, then it cannot be twisted and misused to justify all sorts of violence.

The pacifist's argument here is obviously specious. The corruption of a principle does not abolish the value of that principle. Eliminating all ethical precepts that could be distorted and abused would leave us without any. However, the reminder that we all face the temptation to manipulate our ethical principles to justify our own desires is quite valuable.

One More Option

What, then, have we determined about the reasonableness of absolute pacifism so far? Is it really an option for the person who desires to lead a morally upright life? We have seen that western religions have no divine commands that demand their followers reject all violence—though they are called to be peacemakers. Also, the argument that violence always makes a situation worse has not been made persuasively. In fact, it is not hard for most of us to think of situations where violence, or the willingness to use violence, has made the world a better place. From the Allies in World War II to my local sheriff's department, I am happy that there have been people who were willing to take up arms, at substantial risk to their own lives, to liberate others and keep them safe.

At the same time, we must recognize that the human proclivity for violence resides deep inside us. We are often too willing to resort to violence too quickly. This leaves most of us, then, in exactly the same place on this essential moral issue. We recognize that it is always unfortunate when violence happens, but there are some times when its use is acceptable—even

---

25. Brimlow, *What About Hitler*, 45.

commendable. Some believe these occasions are very rare, while others see the utility of violence more readily. But that is a question of particulars. The underlying ethic is the same: violence is sometimes acceptable to achieve a greater good.

There are individuals, however, who may agree with this principle, but still choose to embrace pacifism. Steven Lee describes them this way:

> Some people regard pacifism as an individual option, a "lifestyle choice," as a principle that should be held only by those who think that it is right for them. This may be referred to as *particularistic* pacifism. For the particularistic pacifist, pacifism is an individual preference, and it does not and should not apply to those who do not prefer it.[26]

There are people who decide, for various reasons, to live a life of non-violence. At the same time, they do not insist that it is a universal moral obligation. They may want to be a symbol of hope, representing what human beings are capable of. They may want to show the world how human beings were intended to live, while not denying the necessity for others to use violence in a fallen world. We may imagine a protester standing in the face of cudgels, water cannons, or a column of tanks and saying, "I oppose you with all that I am, but I will not oppose you with violence." Such a person may not categorically reject violence by all people at all times, but she may have decided to make her life a symbol of peace.

There is an aesthetic appeal to this, a romantic notion that is attractive to many. However, such a person requires two very important attributes: 1) tremendous courage; and 2) the humility to acknowledge that others' willingness to use violence is what makes her statement possible.

The need for courage is obvious,[27] the latter less so. For those who would choose such a life, they are in need of others who bear the sword. Without the latter, their personal security, education, occupation, property, and right to speak could never have been achieved. If you or I were to live such a life, we would need to recognize that we have the privilege to do so because of so many others who bear arms to create order in our society. The moment we feel morally superior to them we become hypocrites, as such an ethic may only exist because of their personal sacrifice.

---

26. Lee, *Ethics and War*, 22.

27. We may speak of courage among pacifists only when there is the possibility that they may actually need to face down violence without resorting to it themselves. Committing oneself to nonviolence while living a comfortable life of privilege, working on a college campus, and never actually facing physical danger, cannot really be considered courageous.

Dietrich Bonhoeffer's sister-in-law Emmi raised a challenge to those who would avoid involvement in the attempt to assassinate Hitler. She wrote to Dietrich in 1939, "You Christians are glad when someone else does what you know must be done . . . but it seems that somehow you are unwilling to get your own hands dirty and do it."[28] While this is not necessarily a rejection of pacifism, her words should trouble anyone who is willing to hand off the responsibility to shed blood.

This brings us back to Clement of Alexandria, the early church father who we discussed at the beginning of this chapter. He saw nonviolence as one lifestyle through which one could live out the Christian life (although admittedly he saw it as superior). Since that time, there have been individuals who have chosen to live by a different ethic of this sort. Monks, nuns, and clergy in Christianity are among those who are sometimes asked to live such a life. Thomas Aquinas (1225–1274) believed that Jesus' command to "Put your sword back in its scabbard" was indeed a call to nonviolence, but as it was directed to Peter, it was only applicable to "bishops and clerics. Consequently, they may not fight."[29] Other members of society are not held to that same exacting standard. We hope, however, that those called to nonviolence remember that their very lives are constantly under the protection of those who must live by a different code.

While such an individual commitment to nonviolence requires courage and humility, it may also require a moral sacrifice that is even harder to make. The willingness to sacrifice oneself for principle is not easy, but the world is full of inspiring examples. Dietrich Bonhoeffer, Jose Rizal, and Maximilian Kolbe happen to be three of my favorite martyrs. Many of us, given the right situation, may have the same mettle within us to gird up our loins and face our own deaths nonviolently. However, would we be prepared to let another die for our moral convictions?

Imagine that I have the power to violently stop, and possibly kill, an aggressor who is not threatening me, but the six-year-old girl who lives down the street. While one may respect, or even seek to emulate, nonviolence that results in my own death, should we make that same decision when it is another's life on the line? Should another die or suffer grievous bodily harm as a result of my principled stand? We can imagine a priest caught in that situation, trying desperately to protect the child by interposing his body, even at risk to his own life. However, what would we think if he let her die, because the only way to stop the assailant was through a use of violence? We may not be comfortable with the image of a priest cracking someone in the

28. As in Metaxas, *Bonhoeffer*, 359.
29. Aquinas, *Summa Theologica* 2a2æ 40, 2.

head with an axe handle, but many of us would demand it if the alternative was the death of an innocent.

Theologians as influential as Saint Augustine (354–430) and Luther have made the argument that Christians should not use force to defend themselves, but are certainly justified (or even required!) in using force to defend their neighbors.[30] Turner explains that for Augustine, "This justification itself follows from charity (caritas), as does the injunction not to resist evil directed at oneself."[31] That is, the command to love means that we should be willing to suffer patiently, but not that we should allow innocent neighbors to suffer when we have power to act. Love of neighbor demands that we act to protect others from injustice, even when it may require violence. Theologian Emil Brunner (1889–1966) expressed the same idea when he wrote, "[The Christian] must do this if he is not to evade the most urgent of all demands of the love commandment, the demand to protect the dyke which saves human life from chaos."[32]

Reinhold Niebuhr summarized this entire issue quite nicely:

> Pacifistic absolutism is sometimes justified by the argument that reverence for life is so basic to the whole moral structure that the sanctity of life must be maintained at all hazards. But even this rather plausible argument becomes less convincing when it is recognized that life is in conflict with life in an imperfect world, and therefore no one has the opportunity of supporting the principle of the sanctity of life in an absolute sense. Fear of the overt destruction of life may lead to the perpetuation of social policies through which human life is constantly destroyed and degraded.[33]

Before concluding this section, I would like to raise one final consideration: the individual principled stand against violence may make sense

---

30. Augustine's mentor Ambrose (c. 340–397) had taught the same thing:

> I do not think that a Christian, a just and a wise man, ought to save his own life by the death of another; just as when he meets with an armed robber he cannot return his blows, lest in defending his life he should stain his love toward his neighbor. The verdict on this is plan and clear in the books of the Gospel. 'Put up thy sword, for everyone that taketh the sword shall perish with the sword.' What robber is more hateful than the persecutor who came to kill Christ? But Christ would not be defended from the wounds of the persecutor, for He willed to heal all by His wounds (On the Duties of Clergy, III.4.27).

31. Johnson, Ethics and the Use of Force, 82.

32. As in Niebuhr, Interpretation of Christian Ethics, 95.

33. Niebuhr, Interpretation of Christian Ethics, 120.

when one's own life is on the line. Perhaps I could refrain from violence if the only life at risk were my own. However, we must recognize that very often our lives are not simply our own. From a utilitarian perspective, I must ask myself if my principled death does more good than harm. Bonhoeffer inspired generations of Christians; Rizal became the father of his country; Martin Luther King Jr. helped bring civil rights to millions of Americans. Their martyrdom inspired countless members of subsequent generations. However, there are situations when a principled stand makes very little positive difference, especially when compared to the cost.

I have a friend who was once attacked by a violent felon with a weapon. He could have set aside his right to self-defense and perhaps been killed. By breaking the man's arm and throwing him to the ground, he was not directly defending anyone else present, as they were not being threatened. He could have been a pacifistic symbol of peace. To be frank, I think very little good would have resulted from that particular principled stand. And I am sure that his family was very happy that he returned home to them that night, safe and sound. Before we encourage or applaud others for a commitment to nonviolence, we must carefully consider the repercussions for themselves, their families, and their communities.

As we have seen, the danger of Christian pacifism can be that an insufficient response is given to evildoers and innocent lives are lost. However, there is one other potential victim of this ethic: the psychological well-being of those who engage in justified violence.

In the introduction of this book, I mentioned Marine Captain Timothy Kudo, who wrote an op-ed for *The Washington Post* in which he detailed how he struggled mightily with a personal demon: "I killed people in Afghanistan. Was I right or wrong?" Not only was he haunted by actions that led to the loss of human life, including the lives of innocents, but he was also troubled by a religious upbringing that had taught him that "killing is always wrong." He had committed no war crimes, nor violated rules of engagement. No one else was questioning his integrity. However, an overly simplistic (and unbiblical) ethic of nonviolence had exacerbated the struggles he had since returning from war. There are those who believe they are doing an unequivocal good by teaching an ethic of nonviolence. However, consideration must be given to the "moral injury" that such an ethic adds to those who may already struggle with the killing they were required to do.

CHAPTER 4

Nonviolence in the East

Non-violence is not a garment to be put on and off at will. Its seat is in the
heart, and it must be an inseparable part of our being.

—Mohandas Gandhi

In Asia, much more so than in the West, we find philosophical and religious traditions that emphasize the ethical importance of nonviolence.
As we have seen, western pacifism is oriented more toward broad social utility—making the world a better place. Asian traditions, on the other hand,
tend to look at violence in terms of its corrupting effect on the individual
committing the act. One finds this ethical value most clearly expressed in
three religions that have their origins in India: Hinduism, Jainism, and
Buddhism. In these three traditions, we find explicit endorsement of the
moral principle known as *ahimsa*. Mahavira (599–527 BCE), the patriarch
of Jainism, expressed this ethical principle by stating that "All breathing, existing, living, sentient beings should not be slain, nor treated with violence,
nor abused, nor tormented, nor driven away. This is the pure, unchangeable,
eternal law."[1]

While adherents of these three religions differ in exactly how *ahimsa*
should be understood, it is agreed that this moral ideal requires more than
pacifism. *Ahimsa* requires that one completely avoid any action of harm or
violence toward any living creature. This ethical principle prohibits killing,
allowing others to kill, the consumption of meat, occupations that cause

1. *Acaranga Sutra* I:4.1, as in Chapple, "Dialectic of Violence," 263.

50

harm (e.g., a fisherman or weapons-maker), and even sports that cause pain and injury. Jainism sets the moral bar so high that even the accidental killing of a fellow creature should be actively avoided. This is the reason that Jains sweep the ground in front of them as they walk, so they do not accidentally step on an insect. Some Jains teach that one should use a filter when collecting drinking water, so as not to kill the small organisms living therein. The moral teaching of *ahimsa*, then, raises the standard of nonviolence much higher than what one generally finds in the West.

Moreover, *ahimsa* is not a matter of interpretation or preference, it is a moral absolute. Buddhism does have moral precepts that are open to negotiation. However, the first precept, which requires one to abstain from "harming living beings," can never be omitted.[2] For Buddhists, this principle is essentially a deontological principle—an absolute moral rule that does not bend to circumstances.

Are there exceptions?

The answer is generally a definitive "no!" As discussed above, Hinduism has stressed the principle of *ahimsa* for two millennia, which has been understood to mean strict vegetarianism and "absolute noninjury."[3] Strict adherence to *ahimsa* is generally understood to allow no exceptions or extenuating circumstances.

Within the Jain tradition, Mahavira taught that one is morally culpable even for having a dream in which one kills a living being.[4] There really is no wiggle room there.

In Buddhism, the prohibition on violence—directly or indirectly—is made very clear. Euthanasia, abortion, and even speaking of death in positive terms are all condemned. In the *Vinaya*, this is clearly stated:

> Should any monk intentionally deprive a human being of life or look about so as to be his knife-bringer, or eulogise death, or incite [anyone] to death saying "My good man, what need have you of this evil, difficult life? Death would be better for you than life"—or who should deliberately and purposefully in various ways eulogise death or incite anyone to death: he is also one who is defeated, he is not in communion.[5]

In Buddhism, the possibility of an enlightened person ever killing another is impossible. In the *Abhidharma*, "the intention to kill is understood

2. Harvey, *Introduction to Buddhism*, 200.

3. The Tamil Veda (c. 200 CE), as in Gier, *Virtue of Nonviolence*, 35.

4. Gier, *Virtue of Nonviolence*, 29.

5. *Vinaya*.iii.72, as in Keown, *Buddhist Ethics*, 108. The *Vinaya* is the extensive text of rules for those living in the *sangha*, or Buddhist community.

as exclusively unwholesome, and the possibility that it might ever be something wholesome promoted by thoughts of compassion is not countenanced . . . [I]t is a psychological impossibility, a psychological contradiction in terms that one should, when motivated by nonattachment, friendliness (and wisdom), intentionally kill another living being."[6]

But, are there exceptions?

Well, yes. It turns out there are quite a lot. While *ahimsa* may be as close to deontological ethics (i.e., absolute moral commands) as one finds in eastern religions, exceptions to this rule seem to be almost commonplace.

The *Bhagavad Gita* is a tremendously influential religious text in Hinduism, wherein Prince Arjuna is instructed by Lord Krishna that he has a religious duty to fight against the enemies of his kingdom (even though they are his relatives!). His primary moral obligation in life is to be a good prince, which means protecting his subjects. This does create an odd tension within Hinduism. Mohandas Gandhi (1869–1948), among others, interpreted this story allegorically, speaking of the battle within one's soul. However, the direct and literal meaning is hard to ignore.

Despite his alternate reading of the *Gita*, Gandhi himself shied away from complete pacifism. He, like Bonhoeffer, believed that if a man is out of control, running amuck at the expense of innocent lives, he should be killed. The person who takes this action, he tells us, should "be regarded a benevolent man."[7] It is unfortunate that the "exigencies of daily life" require us to violate the vow of nonviolence more than some would like to admit.[8]

Even among the zealous Jains, exceptions could be made. Whereas the Jain king held responsibility for the well-being of his subjects, and ensuring this without a military is probably impossible, a warrior class developed within the Jain community for the purpose of safety in the kingdom.[9] Jains have also been permitted to fight in self-defense.[10]

Chinese history is chockfull of stories of violent Buddhists, "monks who freely indulged in carnage and butchery and took an active part in military expeditions of every description, thus leaving no doubt that warfare was an integrate part of their religious profession for centuries."[11] For example, at the end of the Southern Song Dynasty, Buddhist monks in the

6. Gethin, "Killing a Living Being," 175.

7. Gier, *Virtue of Nonviolence*, 54.

8. Gier, *Virtue of Nonviolence*, 38. Gandhi even allowed for euthanasia in extreme cases (Gier, *Virtue of Nonviolence*, 54).

9. Dundas, *Jains*, 118–20.

10. Gier, *Virtue of Nonviolence*, 29.

11. Jerryson, "Introduction," 3.

Jiangxi province fought against the Mongols. They carried flags that read, "In times of danger, we become generals; once the matter is resolved, we become monks once more." Unfortunately, contrary to their predictions, they were killed in battle.[12]

More famously, monks from the Ch'an sect of Buddhism (known as Zen in Japan) have long had the greatest reputation for fighting and warfare. While stories about the adventures of warrior monks at the Shaolin Temple are often fiction, there was indeed a great deal of martial arts being taught, studied, and utilized at this famous location, which Meir Shahar has well documented.[13]

While Japanese monks did not go to war with the regularity of their Chinese counterparts, there is no denying that many of them were involved in military activity.[14] Sri Lanka, also, still finds Buddhists defending their religious ideals and identity with violence.[15] Even Tibetan Buddhism, which most westerners associate with the Dalai Lama, has a history of violence between rival sects.[16]

Within Buddhist literature, one finds multiple examples of sanctioned violence. For example, while suicide had been clearly condemned from the beginning, we find stories of bodhisattvas[17] who sacrifice their lives for the good of others. The *Vakkali Sutra* tells the story of a saintly follower of the Buddha who ended his life by slitting his own throat, at which moment he attained nirvana.

As time went by, explicit justifications for violence began to appear. The *Mahāprajñāpāramitopadeśa* teaches that murder is not even possible, as people's nature is inherently empty. Human beings do not have a self to kill. Their death is like the ending of a dream.[18] Thus, a philosophical loophole of sorts was discovered and used to argue that one need not worry about ending the life of another being, because such an act is actually impossible.

This brief overview only gives a glimpse of the violence that one finds practiced and sanctioned among religions dedicated to the moral principle of *ahimsa*. How is this possible? The answer is found by considering why these religions embraced *ahimsa* in the first place.

12. Demiéville, "Buddhism and War," 31.

13. Shahar, *Shaolin Monastery*.

14. Brian Victoria has documented this extensively, most notably in his two books *Zen at War* and *Zen War Stories*.

15. See Bartholomeusz, "In Defense of Dharma," 1–16.

16. See Maher, "Sacralized Warfare."

17. Compassionate beings, nearing enlightenment, who dedicate themselves to helping others.

18. Demiéville, "Buddhism and War," 20.

Why *Ahimsa*?

The principle of *ahimsa* did not appear based on a divine command. There was no God or divine figure in these religions who proclaimed that all followers should adhere to an ethic of absolute nonviolence. In Hinduism, we even have Lord Krishna instructing Prince Arjuna to kill his enemies, if we take the story literally.

Justifications for *ahimsa* are also, generally speaking, not utilitarian. Early teachings in these traditions are not based on the idea that violence fails to solve problems. No one was saying that we could achieve the greatest good for the greatest number if the faithful would forsake violence.

Admittedly, there have been religious leaders who have believed that nonviolence in particular situations will achieve this, as Gandhi did while fighting for Indian independence.[19] The Dalai Lama, interestingly, has argued that violence might conceivably restore Tibetan independence, but something else even more valuable would be lost:

> Ours is a civilization that for a thousand years has been dedicated to nonviolence, compassion, and forgiveness, and therefore we struggle for our rights as a people within the parameters of these principles. If we were to abandon them and regain our land through hatred and violent means the loss would far outweigh the gain. The Tibet that we would get back would no longer be the Tibet for which we are struggling. We would have an outer victory, but an inner defeat.[20]

For the most part, opposition to acts of violence in these Asian traditions comes from the belief that harming other living beings harms ourselves. This damage to oneself occurs in two fundamental ways: 1) injury to another is injury to oneself because of the interconnectedness of all life; 2) committing an act of violence degrades the character of the person who causes harm to another.

When all of life—indeed all of existence!—is interconnected, then harm to any one part constitutes harm to all. With all life existing as individual manifestations of the Divine (as in Hinduism), or essentially interpenetrating one another because of its inherent emptiness (as in Buddhism), we cannot harm another without harming ourselves. The Buddhist *Avatamsaka Sutra* provides a helpful image to explain this. The universe can be conceived of as the "jewel-net" of the god Indra. "[E]ach jewel in the net

---

19. At the same time, Gandhi believed that *satyāgraha* ("soul force") would always win over brute force, which may be a bit overly optimistic.

20. Stevens, *Philosophy of Aikido*, 24.

reflects every other one, including their reflections of each jewel, and so on to infinity."[21] Thus, damage to any other individual is reflected throughout our interconnected cosmos. While it may be true that there already exists a great deal of damage, the moral imperative is that we not add to it.

Additionally, there is a direct effect on our own individuality when we cause pain and suffering to other living beings. The necessary mindset required to commit an act of violence is injurious to the self. Gandhi explained, "Violence is simply not possible unless one is driven by anger, by ignorant love and by hatred. The [*Bhagavad*] *Gītā*, on the other hand, wants us to be incapable of anger."[22] Buddhism shares this view of human psychology. Violence cannot take place without anger, aggression, or hatred. This mindset, known as *dvesa* (or aversion), is one of the "three poisons" in the world that leads to suffering. It must be counteracted with *advesa* (non-aggression) and *mettā* (loving kindness).

Proper cultivation of the self, then, requires more than avoiding violence. It demands genuine love for one's attacker. "Gandhi frequently reminds us that true *ahimsā* towards an attacker must combine physical nonretaliation with love and compassion. (In other words, mere passivity without the proper disposition is not necessarily *ahimsā*.)"[23]

If this is the origin and root of the religious ethic of *ahimsa*, then we can better understand all of the exceptions that play out in Hinduism, Jainism, and Buddhism. The ultimate goal in these traditions is to cultivate oneself—body, mind, and spirit—until one reaches enlightenment.[24] Such an occurrence is quite rare, and is usually the result of many lifetimes. As a result, the vast majority of people practicing these religions are not working toward such a goal in this lifetime, but are oriented toward living a good-enough life to have a good reincarnation. Thus, while the moral ideal is indeed *ahimsa*, with all the strictness that it requires, most religious practitioners are not currently attempting to live by such a lofty standard.

If enlightenment is the immediate goal of only a few, and if the majority only aspire to a level of moral uprightness that will ensure a good rebirth, then we can see why there are so many exceptions: the moral ideal exists only for the few. Others need not—and in many situations cannot!—live by the highest standards.

Consider a Hindu day-laborer working in Calcutta, struggling to feed and clothe his wife and children. He is familiar with the ethic of *ahimsa*,

21. Harvey, *Introduction to Buddhism*, 119.

22. As in Gier, *Virtue of Nonviolence*, 37.

23. Gier, *Virtue of Nonviolence*, 34.

24. This point may also be referred to as moksa, nirvana, liberation, or awakening.

but if someone gives him a chicken, he is going to take it home and eat that chicken with his family. They need the protein! And no one would fault him for it. While technically not in accord with *ahimsa*, his life does not afford him the luxury of living by such lofty moral ideals. If he is a man of moral and religious integrity in this life, perhaps his next life will allow him the possibility to pursue a higher level of virtue.

It is no different with other forms of violence. Lord Krishna instructed Prince Arjuna to forge ahead into battle, as his station in *this* life was to be a prince. Just as a farmer, merchant, and baker have religious obligations—to dedicate themselves to their calling, aspiring to carry out their occupations with excellence—so does the prince. Of course, the prince must engage in violence to do his job. Thus, he will not have the opportunity to live up to the highest moral ideal in this life. However, a good job this time around means a good reincarnation, and maybe then he can live in greater accord with *ahimsa*.

Consider the case of warrior monks. Not every Buddhist monastic is trying to attain the highest goal of enlightenment in this lifetime. A monastery might hold only a few individuals who dedicate their lives to the attainment of nirvana. Others are happy to live in support of them, taking care of other responsibilities—from cooking to security. Monasteries were full of a variety of different characters of various religious sensibilities. Demiéville discusses this diversity, pointing out that, in addition to devout Buddhist clergy, one finds others as well: "atypical monks were vagabonds, hermits, deserter soldiers, farmers cheating on their taxes, ecclesiastical employees, and the entire population of what's called 'peasant monks.'"[25] In Japan, one eventually found a division between those who dedicated themselves to their studies and religious discipline (*gakuryo, gakushō*) and a second tier of monks (*shuto*) who served in military positions.[26]

In addition to the division of caste and calling, it is hard to ignore the fact that sometimes violence seems the most compassionate response to a situation. The practical arguments of utilitarians are hard to ignore. Swearing off violence can lead to some really bad situations, and how can a religious person with a heart for others ignore that fact? For this reason, we find the Buddhist paragons of compassion, the *bodhisattva*, sometimes getting involved in violence themselves to help others. In the *Yagacarabhumi*, we are taught that sometimes *bodhisattvas* have a duty to murder, if doing so prevents the victim from carrying out the same crime. It is better to sin oneself, than to allow another to commit that same sin—even when this

25. Demiéville, "Buddhism and War," 35.
26. Demiéville, "Buddhism and War," 35.

means that one will go to hell[27] as a punishment. The *Upayakausalya Sutra* even tells the story of how the Buddha, during a previous life when he was known as "Great Compassion," killed a man who was about to murder five hundred *bodhisattvas*. In these situations, Buddhists commend the sacrifice of the one who sins, incurring guilt and punishment in the place of the other, and therefore this same action also accrues great merit.

Compassion for others has led Buddhists and Hindus to work hard to find ways around the practice of *ahimsa*. In Hindu texts, the king is sometimes understood as the representation of Yama, Lord of Death and Dispenser of Karmic Outcomes. In this position, the use of the death penalty can be understood as an act of beneficence, as the "victim is benefited through relief of karmic burden."[28] In Buddhism, the *Maharatnakuta Sutra*, written more than a thousand years after the death of the Buddha, contains an alleged teaching of his that sometimes killing can be a morally right act, even the killing of the Buddha! After all, the Buddha is empty of substance, so how could one kill him?[29]

On the one hand, it is easy to sympathize with practitioners of these religions who want to provide justification for violence, when violence appears to be the most compassionate action one can take in certain circumstances. However, these mental gymnastics are certainly problematic. Discussing the Buddhists, Demiéville writes,

> Men are made in such a way that they need reasons to justify bending their principles. Consequently, when they eschew a bad habit, it too often comes back, masked as a virtue. Buddhists have taken many alternative routes trying their utmost to legitimize many habits that run completely counter to the Buddhist precept of no-killing.[30]

Karma and Science

It is tempting for we who are not Hindus, Jains, or Buddhists to dismiss all this talk of *ahimsa*. If we do not belong to these traditions, what relevance do they have for our lives? It is easy to conclude that the principle of *ahimsa* has no significance or applicability in the ethical frameworks of westerners.

---

27. The various hells in eastern religions, like Buddhism, are not eternal, but they are pretty miserable places to spend a few thousand years.

28. Jenkins, "Making Merit," 65.

29. Demiéville, "Buddhism and War," 42.

30. Demiéville, "Buddhism and War," 38.

I think, however, that would be a mistake.

Even if we do not accept the religious authority of Mahavira or the Buddha, or believe in reincarnation, there is an important lesson here. Whether or not one believes in karma, we all recognize that the effects of violence do not end when the blow is struck or the physical wounds heal.

Robert "Bobbie" Evan Brown Jr. (1907–1971) was one of America's most remarkable soldiers. At the age of fifteen, he lied about his age and joined the US Army. Despite having only a seventh grade education, he distinguished himself as remarkable soldier, boxer, and football player. With the entry of the United States into World War II, he fought first in North Africa, receiving battlefield promotion to Second Lieutenant. He was then transferred to the 1st Infantry Division, landed at Normandy on D-Day, and fought across France. On October 8, 1944, on Crucifix Hill, Brown destroyed three pill boxes on his own with pole and satchel charges. After recovering from his injuries, he returned to the field, fighting in Czechoslovakia. After the war, he was awarded the Medal of Honor, and continued to serve in the Army until 1952.

While his story is the stuff of adolescent dreams and fantasy, being a war hero is not usually what we imagine it to be. Brown never recovered psychologically from the hell he saw (and participated in) while in Europe. He finally found a job as a janitor at the US Military Academy at West Point. On November 8, 1971, he held a gun to his chest and pulled the trigger.

General William Tecumseh Sherman famously wrote in a letter, "I am sick and tired of war. Its glory is all moonshine. It is only those who have neither fired a shot nor heard the shrieks and groans of the wounded who cry aloud for blood, for vengeance, for desolation. War is hell." That "hell" does not end when the soldier goes home or the enemy surrenders.

In 1995, David Grossman published a fascinating and influential book entitled *On Killing: The Psychological Cost of Learning to Kill in War and Society*. He begins with the observation, well-supported by military historians, that psychologically healthy people simply do not want to kill other human beings. While we often talk and posture as if we are capable of such things, even fooling ourselves, the reality is that the vast majority of people do not really want to kill.

US Army Brigadier General S. L. A. Marshall documented that in World War II, only 15 to 20 percent of American riflemen would actually fire at the enemy during combat.[31] The rest would find all manner of activities to busy themselves with in order to avoid shooting other human beings. Marshall wrote, "[T]he average and healthy individual . . . has such

---

31. Grossman, *On Killing*, 4.

an inner and usually unrealized resistance towards killing a fellow man that he will not of his own volition take life if it is possible to turn away from that responsibility . . . At the vital point [the soldier] becomes a conscientious objector."[32]

This reality leads us to two very important implications for our consideration of ethics and violence: 1) enabling a soldier to kill enemy combatants often requires significant psychological conditioning; 2) the killing that takes place in combat can take a serious psychological toll on the one committing the act of violence, regardless of its moral justifiability.

To help soldiers overcome their natural reticence to kill another human being, militaries in the twentieth century have formulated all manner of training stratagems to enable such violent behavior. (Grossman discusses this at great length in his book.) Conditioning young men and women to fire at images of enemy soldiers, instead of silhouettes, was one tactic. Military cadences that glorify killing and slaughter were another. Finding ways to dehumanize the enemy is also important when trying to overcome our natural aversion to killing. The Nazis did this to great effect, with descriptions of Jews and Russians as subhumans and animals. Indeed, every military that has used slurs to describe the enemy population (e.g., Krauts, Japs, Ragheads, Gooks) has done the same thing.

In describing these tactics, I am not making any moral judgments. An army that will not kill the enemy is a serious danger to the well-being of the nation they serve. Some of this psychological conditioning is obviously necessary. However, it is unfortunate that we must condition young men and women to find killing less objectionable than their natural inclinations would lead them. The task of converting a nation's young adults into effective killers might be necessary for the survival of that nation, but it does come at a cost—our natural, normal, and healthy reticence to kill.

If the effect of pre-combat conditioning on the psyche of young men and women is a concern, much greater is the post-combat struggle, where soldiers must come to grips with their actions on the battlefield. Of course, such an experience is not unique to military personnel. Recently, I was catching up with a friend who serves as a police officer in Ohio. During the conversation, we were talking a bit about his line of work. While he loves his job, and carries it out with integrity, we discussed how people who work full-time in fields that are consistently violent are changed by what they do. It is important to point out that this is often no less true for the homeowner who shoots an intruder in self-defense.

---

32. As in Grossman, *On Killing*, 29.

Grossman argues this: "With the proper conditioning and the proper circumstances, it appears that almost anyone can and will kill."[33] This is true of those serving in the military, law enforcement, and civilians. However, enabling someone to kill does not translate into helping them deal with the psychological repercussions of taking another's life.

The substantial impact of conditions like PTSD on the psychiatric casualties of war is generally recognized, even if not fully understood. However, as Grossman argues at length, the psychological trauma sustained by veterans of foreign wars is not due primarily to extended periods of exposure to danger, or witnessing horrific violence up close and personal. The most significant cause of psychological distress is the killing of other human beings. Moreover, the closer one is to the "enemy" when the act of violence is committed, the greater the trauma.

Personnel who are exposed to the same dangers and horrors of war, but do not look people in the eye and kill them, do not experience the same struggles as those who do. Medics, for example, fall into this category.[34] "Nonkillers are frequently exposed to the same brutal conditions as killers, conditions that cause fear, but they do not become psychiatric casualties."[35] One also finds this phenomenon with officers, who are generally not directly involved in killing,[36] as well as those involved in reconnaissance behind enemy lines.[37]

Those who kill, but do so from a distance, also insulate themselves from some psychological damage. Serving on a naval destroyer during World War II was dangerous and involved killing lots of people. However, "in the twentieth century, psychiatric casualties during naval warfare have been nearly nonexistent."[38] Navy personnel on ships destroy planes, other ships, and land forces. Logically, they understand they are killing people, but the greater physical distance translates into greater emotional distance.

As I have reflected on this, I find myself thinking of my own father. He served as an infantryman in the 157th Regiment of the 45th Infantry Division during World War II. He survived the beaches at Anzio, the brutality of Aschaffenburg, the loss of his comrades at Reipertswiller, and fought in many other battles. His jeep once hit a mine, and then came to rest within

33. Grossman, *On Killing*, 4.

34. Grossman, *On Killing*, 62. "The medic takes not his courage from anger. He runs the same or greater risks of death and injury, but he, or she, is given over on the battlefield not to Thanatos and anger, but to kindness and Eros."

35. Grossman, *On Killing*, 54.

36. Grossman, *On Killing*, 64.

37. Grossman, *On Killing*, 60.

38. Grossman, *On Killing*, 58.

one inch of the detonator on another. In Nuremberg, a sniper's bullet pinged his seat right between his legs.[39] As if that was not enough for any teenager, he was present at the liberation of Dachau Concentration Camp, a description of which is not necessary here.

After exposure to that level of fear, violence, brutality, torture, and death, it is remarkable that my father was not one of the many "psychiatric casualties" of the war. However, he had a number of things going for him, which, if Grossman is right, may explain his mental health. My father held a number of assignments during his time in the infantry. His first exposure to combat was as an ammunition carrier for a .30 caliber machine gun. He also served as a mortarman for a time, as well as a forward observer with a massive radio strapped to his back—a very dangerous assignment. He was then fortunate enough to serve in I-Company as the German-English interpreter for his CO, although he was still "in the shit" during that time as well. In these positions he was in constant danger, witnessing the death of friends and civilians, along with plenty of enemy soldiers. He was also likely involved in the killing of German soldiers, directly and indirectly. However, he never found himself in the position of having to look a man in the eye and kill him.

The absence of that one act may have been what enabled him to cope with all that he saw during his time with the 45th in Italy, France, and Germany. It is the act of killing another human being up close, with its true nature laid bare, that we human beings generally find so appalling, so disturbing, so debilitating. Intense personal violence carries with it far more psychological distress and pain than we typically imagine, and certainly more than we see on television and in the movies.

To extend this even further, Grossman points out that what is far more difficult than *shooting* another human being at close range is *stabbing* him. Bayonet training has long been a staple of military preparedness, but our natural repulsion to this act far exceeds our resistance to pulling a trigger. Evidence from research on Civil War battles shows that soldiers were far more likely to strike an enemy with the butt of their rifles, or swing the barrel of the gun like a baseball bat, than impale them. "[T]he resistance to killing with the bayonet is equal only to the enemy's horror at having this done to him."[40]

Lastly, he points out that what is even more difficult than driving a bayonet through a man's body is to get even closer and carry out the act with a knife. He relates the story of one World War II infantry veteran who

39. These latter two stories are detailed in Kershaw, *Liberator,* 190 and 254.
40. Grossman, *On Killing,* 122.

had killed a number of enemy combatants, but was haunted for years with nightmares of the man whose throat he slit. "The horror associated with pinning the man down and feeling him struggle and watching him bleed to death is something that he can barely tolerate to this very day."[41]

Even when we can morally justify our actions, there is a psychological effect that often follows extreme acts of violence. Robert Meagher discusses this in his book *Killing From the Inside Out*, where he speaks of a sense of moral defilement from engaging in such acts, which he likens to the ancient Greek notion of *miasma*.[42]

The reason for this lengthy treatment of the psychological effects of killing, and its relationship to the ethical principle of *ahimsa*, is important. We often imagine that committing an act of grave violence can be carried out, and the only consequences are physical and/or legal. There is the possibility that the other person, or I myself, may be injured and killed, but we forget that acts of brutal violence are contrary to our nature and carry with them a significant psychological impact.

I have trained in countless martial arts schools over the past three decades. Very often I find that people describe maiming or killing techniques—with or without weapons—with no apparent appreciation for the brutality they are simulating. How to shatter a clavicle, crush a trachea, or break a neck are described in the same way as a tennis coach describes how to follow through with a backhand. Often, these subjects are presented as play and met with delight and joking. To be honest, I have engaged in this as well. To be fair, some of this is done to create emotional distance. However, behind the casual way that martial artists describe brutal violence, there must be recognition of the wretchedness of what is being described. And when instruction gets to the point of romanticizing such violence, a good teacher needs to pause and set the record straight.

We must remember that, for most of us, our exposure to violence is limited to what we see on the screen, or what we emulate in martial arts classes. In both cases, the enemy is vanquished, and the champion calmly walks away, ready for whatever may be next. In reality, committing the acts we see carried out so effortlessly in the movies or in video games leaves a heavy emotional toll on normal healthy people. John Keegan and Richard Holmes tell the story of an Israeli paratrooper who found himself face-to-face with an enemy combatant from Jordan. It was simply a kill-or-be-killed situation, happening in the instant. The Israeli recounted, "I moved the Uzi,

41. Grossman, *On Killing*, 130.

42. Meagher, *Killing from the Inside Out*, 42. Meagher offers an interesting insight by differentiating moral fault and moral pollution, but ultimately fails to develop the idea, instead compromising his entire project by dismissing just war theory altogether.

slowly, slowly it seemed, until I hit him in the body. He slipped to his knees, then he raised his head, with his face terrible, twisted in pain and hate, yes such hate. I fired again and somehow got him in the head. There was so much blood . . . I vomited, until the rest of the boys came up."[43]

What we see here is that the insight of Hindus, Jains, and Buddhists is right. Committing acts of violence has a corrupting effect on our psyche. If one's religious goal is to cultivate oneself mentally and spiritually to the point of absolute mental equanimity, health, and well-being, it is easy to see how committing acts of violence can be a serious impediment to achieving such a goal. The person who has the privilege to live in accord with *ahimsa* has far fewer impediments as she seeks to cultivate her virtues. Committing acts of violence can easily inhibit the cultivation of our well-being and virtue.

This is certainly not to say that individuals who have engaged in violence are emotionally or spiritually stunted. By no means! However, violent acts can result in trauma that may interfere with our psychological health. In these three Asian religions, the ultimate goal of human existence is to attain to the highest level of self-cultivation—overcoming all delusion, anger, and lust. The act of violently ripping the life out of another human being— even when completely justified—can certainly be an obstacle to that goal.

Jainism teaches that our moral actions produce physical "particles of karma" that adhere to a person when she commits an immoral act, like engaging in violence.[44] These particles weigh us down and prevent our true nature from shining through. Hinduism and Buddhism have similar understandings, although the karmic residue is not understood as physical. Whether or not one accepts the existence of karma, the image is helpful. There are actions we take that weigh us down, that darken our inner light. Even when those actions may have been necessary, like the World War II veteran who slit a man's throat, or the Israeli with the Uzi, they do have a harmful impact on us as individuals. They can interfere with our ability to cultivate ourselves unimpaired, and flourish mentally and spiritually.

There is a moral conundrum here, though, that must be pointed out. If the goal of self-cultivation is to be of service to others, how do we understand the place of self-sacrifice? Can I sacrifice my own character development in order to be of greater service to another human being? You can see the paradox. The individual who develops mentally, spiritually, emotionally, and ethically will become more compassionate. At the same time, an act of genuine charity or love is often a self-sacrificing act. Thus, committing an

---

43. Keegan and Holmes, *Soldiers*, cited in Grossman, *On Killing*, 114.

44. Chapple, "Dialectic of Violence," 265.

act of violence may be an act of compassion for another, but destructive to oneself.

If executing a criminal was in the best interest of one's society, would you volunteer to swing the axe?[45] Could you accept the personal burden of doing so, for the sake of law and order in society? Should you volunteer for military service to save another the pain of doing so, but bear the pain yourself? Would you personally kill thousands of men in order to save your nation? I wonder if Fa Mulan had nightmares after the battle at Tung Shao Pass.[46]

This is what we have already seen with the compassionate *bodhisattvas*, discussed above, who killed criminals who were on their way to commit atrocities, in order to spare them the karmic punishment they would otherwise incur. Suffering for others, whether by sacrificing one's own life, freedom, or mental health, is the height of compassion. And so, while personally committing acts of violence may impede one's character development, doing so for the sake of another can constitute a response to a higher calling.

Perhaps, then, this Asian perspective on violence tells us something we already know. Acts of violence are always dreadful. They harm the victims, and they harm the ones committing the act. A lifetime that is spared of violence is the most blessed, and we have a moral obligation to work toward that end—for ourselves and others. However, this world of delusion, greed, and anger does not permit us all to live such a life. For the sake of justice, compassion, and mercy, there are situations where individuals feel called to violence. At times with anguish, such destructive acts are undertaken, with the hope that subsequent violence and suffering will be reduced. In the midst of suffering, there abides the hope of a future when we are spared of this misery.

I recently heard a retired police officer speak at my teenage son's graduation from Camp Cadet. He explained to the young men and women that police have no desire for violence, but it's a "necessary evil." I have heard this description of violence many times, but I'm not sure that "evil" is the

---

45. This example may be anachronistic, as we now have secure prisons and good alternatives to beheading. However, for most of human history those two things did not exist. Such a question may seem irrelevant for us today, but it was not for many people for thousands of years.

46. Admittedly, I am having some fun with a fictional account here. However, personal responsibility for the deaths of thousands in order to keep one's homeland from invasion does not reside in fiction alone. What the storytelling usually leaves out, though, is the personal anguish and guilt that may follow for the rest of one's life.

appropriate word.[47] Hindus, Buddhists, and Jains do not describe violence as evil. As we have seen in the discussion of Western pacifism and Eastern *ahimsa*, violence is unfortunate, damaging, and too often self-perpetuating. However, an act committed for the greater good of one's neighbors cannot be described as evil. Reinhold Niebuhr critiques the "middle classes and the rational moralists," who "are wrong in their assumption that violence is intrinsically immoral. Nothing is intrinsically immoral except ill-will and nothing intrinsically good except goodwill."[48] Just as acts of violence or in-action can both be morally reprehensible, so too can they serve the common good. Determining what action is morally right is always a tremendous challenge, but categorical rejections of the use of force have never held up under scrutiny or sustained practice.

This brings us, I suppose, to the same place where we finished our treatment of western pacifism. Violence is, by definition, destructive. Human societies *should* exist without human beings causing harm to one an-other, and the presence of such actions indicates that something has already gone wrong. Moreover, we moral creatures have an obligation to facilitate peace wherever we can.

However, any universal commitment to nonviolence will inevitably run up against the utilitarian reality that sometimes, for some people, in some circumstances, the use of violence becomes an act of compassion. Very often, that compassion is directed toward the innocent, when we place their physical welfare above that of someone who would do them harm. At other times, compassion may be directed toward the target of the violence, as when a police officer chooses non-lethal, rather than lethal, force when given the choice.

In the end, we see that the various justifications for absolute nonvio-lence break down when charity demands that we act violently toward the guilty to save the innocent. This is what we must remember within a critical examination of Eastern and Western arguments for absolute nonviolence. At the same time, the presence of people with such ethical convictions greatly serves our societies as well, as they model for us what a commitment to peace can look like. Moreover, they demand of us the strongest justifications for violence and thereby curb the hawkish inclinations that often exist in our societies. While I cannot accept their ethics, I maintain a respect for the boldness of their convictions and the value they bring to a civilized society.

47. For example, Waller goes so far as to define evil as "the deliberate harming of humans by other humans" (*Becoming Evil*, 13).

48. Niebuhr, *Moral Man and Immoral Society*, 170.

PART THREE

Just War Theory

I am sick and tired of war. Its glory is all moonshine. It is only those who have neither fired a shot nor heard the shrieks and groans of the wounded who cry aloud for blood, for vengeance, for desolation. War is hell.

—William Tecumseh Sherman

The idea of religion-sanctioned violence can make many of us uncomfortable. There are far too many cases—historical and contemporary—where deplorable acts of violence have been committed in the name of religion. The shocking disconnect between the teachings of a religion and the acts of its adherents can leave us horrified, and rightfully so.

We have already considered those who eschew all violence on the basis of their faith. Many other religious people are not pacifists, but speak of violence as a "necessary evil." Even those who believe violence is sometimes justified remain ill-at-ease with the idea that these acts might be charitable, let alone required of us by the will of God. Any time an act of violence receives a religious imprimatur, we get nervous. However, our initial reactions may not actually be in line with more reasoned conclusions. Violence committed with religious sanction is not always the appalling deed we imagine. In fact, the idea is not that radical at all.

Saint Thomas treats the question of war within his chapter on the virtue of love, or *caritas*. This may be surprising. We usually associate a refusal to act violently with love. However, we reside in a fallen world, where choosing nonviolence can expose others to even greater violence. A failure to act, or ineffective efforts, can cause my neighbor far more harm than good. We must choose between relative goods that affect multiple people, and I must take the well-being of all into account. H. David Baer points out, "Jesus may have told his disciples to turn the other cheek, but he did not tell them to lift up the face of their neighbor so that it might also be struck."[49] Love may require dreadful actions.

Imagine walking down the street, talking to your priest on your cell-phone. As you turn the corner, you find a large man severely beating a child. You immediately try to intervene with words and nonviolent actions—try-ing to pull the man off the child. For whatever reason, this fails to deter the man's actions, which are increasingly life-threatening to the child. You then spot a two-by-four lying on the ground next to the man. Would you leave the board on the ground, and continue your pleading with the assail-ant? Could you decide that this situation *might* permit violence, but then choose not to get involved, and walk away? Would your priest, overhearing the situation, discourage the use of violence? Or might he yell over the line, "For the love of God! Hit him in the head!" Would you smash the guy on the head, knowing that such a blow could conceivably be fatal, in order to save the life of the child? This decision could easily and sincerely be justified as following the divine command to take up the cause of the oppressed and powerless. Continuing to attempt peaceful but ineffective measures to ease your conscience would not be praiseworthy.

As unfortunate as it is, we live in a world where violence can be an act of compassion; where the requirement to defend the widow and orphan cannot always be met without the dreadful presence of violence. My favorite charitable organization, the International Justice Mission, works with police to liberate young girls who have been trafficked into prostitution. That does not happen without the presence of firearms, nor could it. Moreover, we must acknowledge that the responsible use of firearms requires the willing-ness to use them.[50] Without a willingness to use violence, their work would be impossible.

The use of violence for the greater good may be practiced by individual citizens, law enforcement, or nation states. In these cases, the ethical ques-tions of when we should use violence and what manner of violence we can use become very important. This is how we struggle to bring our actions in line with our ethical convictions—convictions which are often rooted in our religious beliefs.

49. Baer, *Recovering Christian Realism*, 31.

50. Anyone familiar with gun safety knows that a person should never carry a fire-arm for protection unless she is actually willing to use it to shoot another human being.

Around the world, leaders within different religious and philosophical traditions have long instructed their adherents in how to fight with virtue. The Hindu *Law of Manu* forbade the use of poison arrows.[51] The Muslim philosopher Averroes (1126–1198) strongly condemned the killing of children and non-combatant women in warfare.[52] Sikh warriors have long abided by strict ethical rules about the treatment of those who surrender. Plato recorded Socrates instructing his countrymen to fight "like people who know one day that they will be reconciled."[53]

It is in the history of Christian nations, however, that we find the tradition known as just war theory. This is not a singular or fixed ethical construct. One can trace the evolution of this theory within the history of Christianity, through the Enlightenment, and into our contemporary context. I believe that understanding just war theory is essential to critical thinking about warfare between nations. It can also help us think about the ethics of interpersonal violence. As such, it will form the framework for our ethical deliberations of personal acts of violence in the following part of this book. To understand "just wars," however, the following chapters will consider both the origins of just war theory and how it has changed over the centuries. We will then conclude by considering aspects of this ethical model that are currently being debated.

51. Lee, *Ethics and War*, 222.

52. Johnson, *Ethics and the Use of Force*, 68.

53. Lee, *Ethics and War*, 38.

CHAPTER 5

Classical Just War Theory

When all efforts to restore peace prove useless and no words avail,
Lawful is the flash of steel. It is right to draw the sword.

—Guru Gobind Singh

Just war theory is generally discussed in terms of two fundamental considerations: determining when going to war is morally justified, and deciding what conduct within warfare is morally acceptable—i.e., *jus ad bellum* and *jus in bello*. We will treat both of these categories in the following pages.

Jus ad bellum

The first consideration when looking at the ethics of war is whether or not it is right to engage in hostilities in the first place. Is one group morally justified in taking up arms against another? This ethical concern is known as *jus ad bellum*, which is Latin for "the right to engage in war." Through most of the history of just war theory, this was the primary (and sometimes only) ethical consideration.

For centuries, there have been various lists of criteria. However, the classical expression of this theory, expressed by Saint Thomas Aquinas in the thirteenth century, contains just three. While we will consider other additional qualifications below, we begin with these three.

For entry into warfare to be just, the military action must be (a) carried out by a proper authority; (b) for a just cause; (c) carried out with good intention, in order to create peace and avoid evil.[1] This, of course, leaves us with many questions. Who is a proper authority? What constitutes a just cause? How does one determine good intention? Thomas discussed these matters at some length, drawing upon Saint Augustine in the process.

Proper Authority

To begin, a just war may only be declared by those who have legitimate authority to bear arms; e.g., the Holy Roman Emperor or the government of a country recognized by the United Nations today. Individual citizens may never call for war. Thomas explained, "[A] private person has no business declaring war . . . [n]or can he summon together whole people, which has to be done to fight a war."[2] Just war theory subsequently denies to purely religious authorities the right to declare war; temporal authorities alone have the "right of the sword." Thus, the idea of a "just war" is not the same as a "holy war."[3] Religious authorities may weigh in on the subject and make suggestions, but they lack the authority to declare war. Thus, according to just war theory, Pope Urban II was exceeding his authority when he called for the First Crusade in 1095.

Just Cause

Traditionally, there were three justifiable causes for war. James Turner Johnson lays these out as "defense of the common good, recovery of something wrongfully taken, and punishment of evildoers."[4] Today, we often think of national self-defense as the primary justification for war. However, as Johnson explains, just reasons for going to war extended beyond a nation defending its borders. The tyrant next door who slaughters a religious or ethnic minority group was a fair target for military action. The broader defense of the public good, both within and beyond one's borders, justified the use of force. Thus, it extended to "defense of the peace and order both of the

---

1. Aquinas, *Summa Theologica,* 2a2æ 40, 1.

2. Aquinas, *Summa Theologica,* 2a2æ 40, 1.

3. Johnson, *Ethics and the Use of Force,* 51. In societies where individuals can hold positions of both religious and political authority, this differentiation breaks down.

4. Johnson, *Ethics and the Use of Force,* 93.

immediate community and of the fundamental structure of order on which all communities depended."[5]

Additionally, a nation does not need to wait until an actual attack has taken place before striking at one's enemies. As Michael Walzer makes clear, "Both individuals and states can rightfully defend themselves against violence that is imminent but not actual; they can fire the first shots if they know themselves about to be attacked."[6] A virtuous nation may not want to throw the first punch, so to speak, but when its enemy has positioned itself to extinguish "peace and order," the threatened party may attack preemptively. Nonetheless, this is a tricky aspect of just war theory.

The case of a pre-emptive attack that is often cited is what happened between Israel and Egypt in 1967. Israel's pre-emptive attack on Egypt at the start of the Six-Day War is generally considered justified because of the military buildup that was happening along its border, along with the imminent violation of its national sovereignty. It is generally agreed upon that Israel would have suffered tremendous loss—perhaps its very existence—if it had waited for Egypt (and allies) to cross Israeli borders. Its best chance at survival, with war looming, was to act first and quickly take out Egyptian airstrips, followed by eliminating its stranded air force. This ensured air superiority throughout the war, which lasted a mere six days!

However, other cases are rarely so clear-cut. Would we condone a similar anticipatory military action by Israel against a neighboring nation who develops a nuclear weapon and threatens to use it "to wipe Israel off the map?" Similarly, were Soviet missiles in Cuba sufficient cause for a first-strike, or America's placing missiles in Turkey? Differentiating between defensive fortification, saber-rattling, and mobilization for war can be quite difficult. Determining the point at which hostilities are certain and inescapable is no easy task. However, when that moment is reached, the obvious advantage in striking first has been understood to be morally justified.

Good Intention

The existence of a just cause for going to war does not automatically sanctify a governing authority's decision to do so. The intent behind the decision must be honorable. In discussing this third requirement, Thomas explains, "[T]hey must intend to promote the good and to avoid evil." He then goes on to quote Augustine: "Among true worshippers of God those wars are looked on as peacemaking which are waged neither from aggrandizement

---

5. Johnson, *Ethics and the Use of Force*, 18.

6. Walzer, *Just and Unjust Wars*, 74.

nor cruelty, but with the object of securing peace, or repressing the evil and supporting the good."[7]

When the United States led a coalition of nations against Iraq in 1991, the just cause was easy to identify: the sovereignty of Kuwait had been violated by the invading Iraqi army. The moral argument that America was undertaking this war for its own selfish reasons, primarily its desire for oil, was a challenge to the "good intention" of the war effort. This objection was thus a claim that this was not actually a just war; it was being carried out for selfish reasons, rather than a genuine desire for peace and justice. Not everyone, of course, has found this argument persuasive, and so I leave it to the reader to reach his or her own conclusions on the subject. It is worth pointing out, however, that we usually make decisions based on multiple considerations. This certainly complicates our efforts to evaluate the genuine "intentions" of ourselves, let alone others.

Jus in Bello

When we consider morally right conduct within war, there are additional concerns. One may enter a war justly, but then conduct it unjustly. Thomas explains, "[I]t is lawful to repel force by force, provided one does not exceed the limits of a blameless defense."[8] Classical just war theory would also develop three rules to govern morality once fighting had begun. As with *jus ad bellum*, additional considerations have been raised over the centuries. However, we begin with the three principles of "discrimination, proportionality, and due care."[9]

Discrimination

This principle demands that military operations discriminate between their targets. Most basically, enemy combatants may be intentionally targeted; non-combatants may not. This differentiation also extends to enemy soldiers engaged in fighting as opposed to those who have surrendered. In the US Army's publication "The Soldier's Rules," the expectations are made clear. "Soldiers fight only enemy combatants. Soldiers do not harm enemies who surrender. Soldiers do not kill or torture enemy prisoners of war."[10]

---

7. Aquinas, *Summa Theologica,* 2a2æ 40, 1.

8. Aquinas, *Summa Theologica,* 2a2æ 64, 7.

9. Lee, *Ethics and War,* 154.

10. As in Johnson, *Ethics and the Use of Force,* 89.

This does not mean, of course, that the US Army does not kill non-combatants during war. Countless civilians have been killed, and will be killed, during military operations that are carried out in keeping with *jus in bello*. What militaries may not do, however, is intentionally seek to kill innocents. Unfortunately, the reality of warfare means that even well-intentioned efforts to target military objectives alone still lead to "collateral damage"; i.e., the unintended death of those we would prefer to spare. Depending on the context, discrimination can be more or less difficult to follow. On the one hand, new technology enables greater discrimination, even if it cannot overcome all killing of innocents. On the other, enemy combatants hiding among civilian populations undermine these efforts, making it harder (and sometimes intentionally so) to discriminate between the two groups.

While this principle of discrimination is easily understood as an absolute rule, the temptation to put it aside is often present, even among military personnel of integrity and good will. There are easily understood utilitarian arguments for ignoring this mandate, at least occasionally. Movies like "Saving Private Ryan" and "Lone Survivor" illustrate the perceived need to harm enemies who surrender. There are also times when military personnel are tempted to torture POW's who have vital information.

With regard to civilians, the matter becomes complex in a variety of ways. Who is and who is not a combatant is not always readily apparent. The differentiation of combatants and non-combatants is not as easy as picking out men in uniform while sparing women and children. Likewise, drawing a line between a military and civilian target is not as easy as looking at a map. Dropping atomic bombs on cities to end a war quickly, and thereby saving hundreds of thousands of lives, looked like the best option to many in 1945. In Hiroshima and Nagasaki, before the bombs fell, large numbers of civilian women and young people were training with spears and *naginata* (glaives) to fight the US soldiers during the expected invasion of the mainland. Whether this was a violation of the principle of discrimination has been a topic of considerable disagreement ever since.

Proportionality

This second principle demands that those directing combat consider the relative damage to the other nation's population and property. Warfare almost always creates a substantial number of casualties, destruction of property, and other considerable losses to the innocent. However, care must be taken to ensure that this does not take place out of proportion to the good sought through warfare.

Imagine if Cuban nationals, supported by their government, detonated a small bomb on an American military base in Florida. The United States would have just cause to respond with military force. Those planning a military response would know that a number of civilian deaths and property damage could likely result from such an action. That might be proportional. The US would not, however, be justified in carpet bombing Havana. Similarly, the occasional calls to bomb some Middle-Eastern country "back to the stone age" because its government supported terrorist attacks would also be a violation of proportionality.

A strong and swift response is generally desirable—one that will deter the aggressor nation as well as others who see the consequences of starting a war. However, while a more violent response creates a greater deterrence, and may create a more peaceful future, it may exceed the (admittedly vague) parameters of proportionality.

Due Care

In a nutshell, the concern here is for the suffering of all involved in war. This final consideration is sometimes broken down into parts—its relation to combatants and non-combatants. While the killing of enemy soldiers is generally assumed (and condoned), the manner in which this is carried out is subject to ethical review. Lee explains, "Moral consideration should be given not just to the killing of combatants, but to their suffering as well."[11] The Hindu prohibition on poison-arrows, discussed above, would fall in this category. The outlawing of chemical and biological weapons also derives from due care, although it overlaps with concerns about discrimination.[12] Johnson sums up this concern of *jus in bello* nicely, writing, "The running themes are two: that weapons of excessive destructive effect and/or weapons whose effects are hard or impossible to control are not to be permitted, and means that are deemed especially indiscriminate, cruel or inhumane are forbidden."[13] Some weapons are unnecessarily severe in the suffering they create, and so efforts must be made to minimize or eradicate their use.

With regard to non-combatants, Protocol I of the Geneva Conventions take up the matter of due care with the following directive: "In the conduct of military operation, *constant care* shall be taken to spare the civilian population, civilians and civilian objects; *all feasible precautions* [shall be

---

11. Lee, *Ethics and War*, 221.

12. O'Donovan treats this prohibition with keen insight in his work *The Just War Revisited*, 78–94 (chapter 3, entitled "Immoral Weapons").

13. Johnson, *Ethics and the Use of Force*, 99.

taken] in the choice of means and methods of attack with a view to avoiding, and in any event to minimizing, incidental loss of civilian life, injury
to civilians and damage to civilian objects."[14] We have already discussed
how indiscriminate acts of violence are not in accord with the *jus in bello*
requirements of just war theory. Here, however, there is the expectation that
combatants must go beyond the requirement to discriminate among targets,
and actively seek to reduce the damage to civilian populations. Lee explains,
"The requirement of precaution is captured in the contrast between *not trying to harm* civilians and *trying not to harm* civilians."[15]

Thus, in one sense, the due care requirement does not discriminate
between combatants and non-combatants. No one should be subject to unnecessary suffering. This obviously leads into discussions of nuclear weapons. It is easy to understand why there are so many people who oppose their
use altogether. After visiting Hiroshima in 2015, I can certainly understand
why the population of that city remains passionate and vocal in calling for
an end to nuclear weapons. The tremendously destructive, indiscriminate,
and cruel effects of that first atomic bomb used in war (relatively small, by
today's standards) is unfathomable. The use of such weapons, according to
some, demonstrates a fundamental lack of care for humanity—both civilian
and military.

The difficulty with the due care requirement is that today's mercy may
be tomorrow's nightmare. There often exists a tension between demonstrat-
ing restraint and prolonging war. Ending a conflict quickly can be the best
solution to a problem at times, as we saw with the Six-Day War. If restraint
prolongs fighting for days, months, or years, such restraint is harder to
qualify as benevolent. With regard to the bombing of Hiroshima, opponents
of the decision must face the utilitarian challenge that one horrific event
that kills a hundred thousand people may be preferable to years of bloody
conflict that result in the deaths of a million.

Similarly, when military targets that are in close proximity to civilian populations are not targeted, for reasons of due care, this can create an
incentive to locate more high value military targets in the middle of such
areas, even right next to schools and hospitals. As such, the challenge of due
care is not simply to be as careful as possible, but to weigh the short- and
long-term benefits of particular actions for the relative good of all.

---

14. As quoted, with emphases, from Lee, *Ethics and War*, 213.
15. Lee, *Ethics and War*, 218.

CHAPTER 6

Just War Theory

Its Historical Development

In stating a single condition of peace, I mean simply to say that the war will
cease on the part of the government, whenever it shall have ceased on the part
of those who began it.

—ABRAHAM LINCOLN

The previous chapter outlined a basic introduction to classical just war theory. However, this ethical construct is not a fixed entity. It has changed over time, exists today in a variety of expressions, and will likely find alternate expressions in the years to come. A brief look over the past centuries can help us understand some of these variations, why they came about, and allow the reader to make judgments about the relative merits of different perspectives.

As we previously examined, early Christians had no need for a developed ethic of warfare. While some believers served in the military, Christians had little political power—or aspiration for it. Decisions about when to go to war, and how to conduct the business of violence, were made by people with no affiliation with the early church.

This changed in the fourth century with the conversion of Emperor Constantine. The Roman world now had a political and military leader who professed the Christian faith. How an empire should conduct itself within a Christian ethical framework became an issue for the first time, and it became serious business. At the end of that century, Emperor Theodosius learned the hard way that the church takes ethics quite seriously. After the "slaughter of Thessalonica," in which seven thousand civilians were killed in response to a relatively small riot, the emperor himself was excommunicated by Saint Anselm, the bishop of Milan. Theodosius had clearly violated the principles of discrimination and proportionality.

Shortly thereafter, it was Saint Augustine who began to discuss the ethics of warfare directly. In fact, he was the first to speak of a "just war," in *The City of God*. While he did not write extensively on the subject, and offered no systematic treatment of the matter, his contributions were significant. He presented an ethical argument that Christians must concern themselves with the good of society, not just their own personal behavior. Johnson explains that Augustine's writing "underscored the idea that a Christian's life in the world in history implies responsibility for assisting in creating and maintaining public order for the sake of justice and peace."[1]

Inspired by his mentor Ambrose, Augustine interpreted the moral commands of Jesus (e.g., "turn the other cheek") to mean that Christians may not use physical force to defend themselves, but they may do so to defend others. A true Christian should be willing to personally suffer all manner of injustices. She may not, however, turn a blind eye to the suffering of others. Christian love, *caritas*, demands that we serve our neighbor. When evildoers would harm or kill them, it is a Christian mandate to step in and help. Augustine was enough of a realist to know that this sometimes requires acts of violence—whether carried out by individuals or nations.

At the same time, charity still extends to one's enemies. While evildoers may sometimes need to be killed, force must be used within appropriate limits. While Augustine did not have the language and categories of *jus in bello* at that time, it is essentially what he was describing. In a letter to Bonifacium he wrote, "We do not seek peace in order to wage war, but we go to war to gain peace. Therefore be peaceful even while you are at war, that you may overcome your enemy and bring him to the prosperity of peace."[2]

The thirteenth century saw significant changes and developments within just war theory. Pope Innocent IV (1195–1254) decreed that "It is permissible for anyone to wage war in self-defense or to protect property. Nor is this properly called 'war' (*bellum*), but rather 'defense' (*defensio*)."[3] The pontiff's point here was not that anyone may declare war in a case of self-defense. Rather, he taught that all people have the right to engage in

1. Johnson, *Ethics and the Use of Force*, 99.
2. As in Aquinas, *Summa Theologica*, 2a2æ 40, 1, ad. 3.
3. As in Johnson, *Ethics and the Use of Force*, 131.

violence to protect themselves and their property. This marks a break with Augustine, who limited such actions to the defense of others.[4]

Thomas Aquinas, during that same century, wrote extensively on the subject. We have already considered his contributions above, as he was instrumental in formulating classical just war theory. In fact, it was his formulation that became the accepted norm for discussing the topic of *jus ad bellum*.[5] We need not revisit his contributions here, but only note that he accepted Pope Innocent's ethic of the moral suitability of self-defense—even for Christians.[6]

It is also important to mention the contributions of the Spanish philosopher and Catholic theologian Francisco de Vitoria (c. 1483–1546). In discussing different types of just wars, he differentiated between "defensive" wars and "offensive" wars. While our initial inclination may be to condemn "offensive" wars, Vitoria was not talking about wars of conquest or aggression. He explained, an offensive war is "war in which vengeance for an injury is sought."[7] Vitoria believed that a war may be justified if it serves a punitive function. Just wars are not limited to self-defense.

Vitoria also differentiated between "vincible ignorance" and "invincible ignorance." He recognized that both sides of a conflict generally believe they are in the right, while at least one must be in the wrong. Vitoria could excuse invincible ignorance, where one could not have perceived the truth correctly. However, vincible ignorance, where one had the ability and opportunity to know the truth, does not excuse one's moral failings. To paraphrase your local district attorney, "Vincible ignorance of the law is no excuse." Or, to quote my mother, "You should have known better."

Vitoria's life overlapped with another influential theologian, Martin Luther. While Luther did not introduce anything new to the debate, his theology contributed to just war theory in more subtle ways. Like Augustine, he insisted that Christians should not resort to violence in self-defense. However, doing so for the safety and well-being of others is an act of love. His understanding of vocation led him to insist that no one's "calling" in this world is superior to another's, as long as one carries it out as a service to God and the community. There is no hierarchy between a priest, a milkmaid, or a soldier; all vocations are God-pleasing if pursued as a means to serve one's neighbor. In *Whether Soldiers, Too, Can Be Saved*, Luther made it clear that

4. Innocent IV did not, however, see just war theory as an extension of the right to self-defense, as Grotius would argue for four hundred years later.

5. Johnson, *Ethics and the Use of Force*, 17.

6. Johnson, *Ethics and the Use of Force*, 82.

7. As in Johnson, *Ethics and the Use of Force*, 52

the calling of a soldier is pleasing to God, insofar as he works to sustain peace in this world. This is not a vocation of necessary evil, but a service to humanity—provided that the soldier performs his duties with virtue, not bloodlust.

Luther famously supported soldiers while condemning rebels/revolutionaries. As a result, he is often judged severely for his failure to support the peasant rebellions of his time. These insurrections were launched by common people in response to blatant abuses committed by the princes. Luther agreed that the princes had acted unjustly, but he could not support these rebellions that were carried out in the name of Christ. According to Luther, the peasants committed three fundamental errors. First and foremost, they violated the first condition of a just war; they were not carried out by legitimate authorities. Second, there was the utilitarian observation that rebellions leave us only with widows and orphans, not a more just and peaceful society. And third, giving a political insurrection the imprimatur of Christ was clearly beyond the teachings of Scripture.[8]

Interestingly, not long thereafter, Lutheran princes faced the moral question of whether they could resist the Roman Catholic emperor. This also appeared to be a violation of the "proper authority" condition. However, through some impressive legal and theological maneuvering, they found ways to justify their armed resistance and claim legitimate authority to do so.

It was Hugo Grotius (1583–1645), the Dutch jurist, who would next play the most significant role in the development of just war theory. The massive bloodshed that took place in fighting between Catholics and Protestants throughout Europe, as in the Thirty Years War which produced about eight million casualties, led to a shift in the interpretation of what constituted *jus ad bellum*.[9] What Europeans discovered was that fighting for the "common good" can be understood to mean fighting against harmful ideas. If that is the case, there is no end to reasons to fight. Eventually, people realized that fighting over competing theologies could lead to perpetual warfare. Thus, the criteria for war shifted to a more modern understanding of nations and borders, where autonomy within another's borders would be respected.

Johnson explains, "The older idea of defense as protection of the common good, under the new understanding of sovereignty, becomes defense

---

8. Luther, "Against the Robbing and Murdering Hordes," 45–56.

9. The Thirty Years War was the historical context for Grotius's *On the Law of War and Peace.*

of the territory and its inhabitants from 'armed attack.'"[10] It is this change which is reflected in the views of many today who regard national self-defense as the only justification for engaging in war. "Grotius's redefined conception of sovereignty removed punishment of heterodox religious belief as a possible cause for use of armed force, and defense of the commonwealth against attack—a defense of its borders, its populace, and its traditions and laws—became the only just cause for use of armed force by the political community."[11] Exactly how much Grotius really changed things is up for debate,[12] but a genuine shift in what determines "just cause" was certainly taking place at this time.

The treaties that led to the "Peace of Westphalia" in 1648 ended both the horrific Thirty Years' War and the Eighty Years' War between the Dutch Republic and Spain. The Treaty of Westphalia, building upon the ideas of Grotius, declared that individual nations hold sovereignty over their own internal affairs. Nations could not intervene in the domestic matters of their neighbors, regardless of how they felt about them. Arms could only be taken up if one country violated the sovereignty of another. Our current understanding of national self-defense as the primary (or only) justification for war is a result of the monumental series of peace treaties that occurred at this time. Johnson explains, "In the idea of just cause the Grotian-Westphalian conception pushes toward ruling out all uses of armed force except in defense, an idea deeply embedded in positive international law as it developed during the twentieth century."[13]

The other major change that Grotius brought was a more intensive consideration of the rules governing the conduct of war, *jus in bello*. This is not to say that this concept was new, but it did not receive much attention until the modern era.[14] For example, his discussion of proportionality demanded that the severity of a military response should not exceed the offense which prompts it. Justice demands that "we ought to do no more to the other than he was prepared to do to us. But there is also no reason to do any less."[15] The idea of proportionality would develop further, to where there would be an attempt to quantify the good accomplished when compared to the harm created, regardless of what the other was "prepared to do."

---

10. Johnson, *Ethics and the Use of Force*, 52.

11. Johnson, *Ethics and the Use of Force*, 133.

12. See Baer, *Recovering Christian Realism*, 37–54.

13. Johnson, *Ethics and the Use of Force*, 52.

14. Lee, *Ethics and War*, 44.

15. As in Johnson, *Ethics and the Use of Force*, 81.

One other issue that was being debated around this time, which deserves much more attention than is permitted in this book, is the question of when a soldier may conscientiously object and refrain from fighting in a particular war which his sovereign has declared. Luther dealt with this issue by advising the following: "If you know for sure that he is wrong, then you should fear God rather than men, Acts 4 [5:29], and you should neither fight nor serve, for you cannot have a good conscience before God." Where matters get tricky, however, is when the just nature of a war is not exactly clear. In such a case, Luther advises this: "But if you do not know, or cannot find out, whether your lord is wrong, you ought not to weaken certain obedience for the sake of an uncertain justice."[16] Vitoria supported this judgment with a more pragmatic concern, arguing, "[I]f subjects were unable to fight until they understood the justice of war, the safety of the commonwealth would be gravely endangered."[17]

Grotius, on the other hand, argues for more restraint on the part of the unconvinced or doubtful soldier. "[W]hoever hesitates, when reflecting, in his decision to act ought to choose the safer course. The safer course, however, is to refrain from war." Even if the act of disobedience to one's sovereign turns out to be wrong, he continues, "[D]isobedience in things of this kind, by its very nature, is a lesser evil than manslaughter, especially than the manslaughter of many innocent men."[18] The morally virtuous soldier should refrain from participating in any war of which he doubts its justice.[19]

Around this time, conversations regarding these matters were shifting away from religious criteria for what constituted a just war and in the direction of secular law. Nevertheless, Grotius differentiated "just" conduct in warfare from what is expected of Christians. God's children are commanded to love one another, even their enemies. This does not mean (as discussed in an earlier chapter) that one cannot kill one's enemies. It does mean that violence should be tempered by mercy and charity, not exercising the full extent of one's rights in a response to aggressors. He cites Saint Thomas to support his claim: "Even under such circumstances the one who is attacked ought to prefer to do anything possible to frighten away or weaken the assailant, rather than cause his death."[20]

---

16. Luther, "Whether Soldiers, Too, Can be Saved," 130.

17. Grotius, *On the Law of War and Peace*, 311. As in McMahan, *Killing in War*, 145.

18. As in McMahan, *Killing in War*, 146.

19. McMahan argues strongly for this position in *Killing in War*, and his examination of this tricky matter is essential reading. Even if one is not fully convinced, his analysis of this ethical dilemma is comprehensive and his argument compelling.

20. Grotius, *On the Law of War and Peace*, 83.

Despite the religious convictions of people like Vitoria and Grotius, just war theory was coming to be based more on natural law than explicitly Christian teaching. That is to say, moral justifications were based less on explicitly religious teachings and more on human reason. Even if the contributions of Christian figures, often expressed in Christian terms, was still commonplace in the discussion, the justifications for the theory became decreasingly dependent on Christian faith. Today, just war theory holds its own weight without appeal to religious authority.

As we reach the twentieth century, new considerations entered the moral debate over what constitutes a just war. The overwhelming carnage brought on by two world wars was unprecedented. At the same time, there were clear cases of moral evil, from Asia to Europe, where armed force was absolutely necessary to avoid a descent into unimaginable darkness. In the latter half of the century, the amassing of weapons that could destroy all life on the planet within twenty-four hours was also a game changer. These three facts have raised considerable questions and challenges that scholars debate as they try to work out an effective ethic of violence for the twenty-first century.

One requirement of *jus ad bellum* that established itself throughout the twentieth century is the "probability of success." Military actions should not be undertaken, according to this principle, if there is not a reasonable expectation of being successful. This appears, in many cases, to be common sense. Wars create unfathomable suffering and destruction. While it has become cliché, it bears repeating that they are "hell." Therefore, unleashing such destruction upon any community, in what is likely to be a futile effort, cannot appear to be morally justified.

Even when the only casualties will be enemy soldiers, there are moral concerns. Are all enemy combatants, particularly those fighting on behalf of an unjust regime, deserving of death? We may *feel* that way, but feelings should not determine ethical matters of such magnitude. Further complicating the matter, different members of the "bad guys" can vary in their moral culpability; for example, the Nazi *Waffen-SS*, as opposed to regular German citizens drafted into the infantry. The former might be deserving of death because of their complicity in the Third Reich, while the latter had little choice in taking up arms. In any case, engaging in a hopeless military operation and killing some enemy combatants, whose spouses and families back home are waiting for them, appears ethically wrong.

In reality, combat almost always affects innocent civilians. This applies to those on both sides of the conflict. Engaging a war with no prospect of success endangers the lives of innocents among the enemy as well as one's own community. The destruction of land, housing, industry, and infrastructure likewise affect noncombatants considerably. If the cause never had a chance, it will be argued that it should never have been undertaken.

However, this additional *jus ad bellum* requirement raises some concerns. To begin with, this principle can be placed under the requirement of "right intention," making it superfluous. If one's intention is to go out in a blaze of glory, or fight to the death on the basis of pride, then "right intention" would already indicate that such a motive is unethical.

There are additional concerns with "probability of success." If the right to engage in war is essentially the same as the human right to self-defense, a position known as "reductive individualism," then both wars and individual use of force (*jus ad vim*) are subject to the same moral rules. We already grant that people may engage in violence in the attempt to protect themselves, even if there is little or no chance of success. Why would it be different in war? A small woman being assaulted by a larger man, intent on killing her, is unlikely to physically overpower him. However, no one would say, therefore, that she has no right to fight with everything she's got until the end.[21] (Doing so in a way that could endanger innocent bystanders is a separate concern, as that would be a question of *jus in bello*.)

The other significant difficulty with the demand for "probability of success" is that one must determine what constitutes "success." In the 1943 Warsaw Ghetto Uprising, Jewish resistance was clearly futile. They were not going to be able to free themselves from the Nazi's impending holocaust. In fact, their efforts led to the earlier demise of thirteen thousand people. Furthermore, they inflicted fewer than three hundred casualties on the Nazis. Was this unsuccessful and therefore immoral? One could certainly argue that they slowed down the Nazi machine, if just a bit, which increased the likelihood of an Allied victory. Furthermore, they were *successful* in inspiring generations of people, around the world and to this day, with their courage and fortitude in the face of evil.

Something similar happened three years earlier when the Norwegian government refused to accept the ultimatum of surrender when Germany offered Norway its "protection." They began their limited resistance, even though it was clear they could not effectively repel the Third Reich. Were they wrong to do so?

We might ask the same of those who fought at Thermopylae. The final stand of the three hundred Spartans, seven hundred Thespians, and four hundred Thebans was clearly going to end with their demise. However, we look to the success in ultimately saving Athens as justifying their march to

---

21. For a different perspective in this issue, see Uniacke, "Self-Defence, Just War," 62–74.

death. One can certainly object that this was a single battle, and not the war. However, the lines that mark the end of a war are not always clear.

Lastly, there have been wars and battles that were fought and won by forces that others regarded as hopeless. From the Battle of Badr to the Siege of Vienna, what may appear to be hopeless can sometimes become a turning point. This begs the following question: how much probability of success must there be to justify the use of force?

In the end, the principle of "the probability of success" is far from clear and agreed upon by just war theorists. Attempting to quantify a specific probability, or define "success," is not easy. While the principle has a certain rhetorical value, and may be helpful in specific contexts, it is problematic as a fixed deontological expectation for a just war. It may have a place as part of conversations about "intent," but it will remain controversial as its own specific requirement.

One of the other changes in the twentieth century was a readiness to describe all violence as wrong, an indication of ill will, or essentially evil. While the roots of this idea can be found in the previous chapters, its expression became more mainstream in the twentieth century: violence may be necessary, but it is a necessary evil. Many Christians, influenced both by the carnage of two global wars, as well as pacifism (eastern and western), began to insist on this new ethic. Others, like Reinhold Niebuhr, objected to this departure from the tradition of Augustine and Thomas. "The one error is the belief that violence is a natural and inevitable expression of ill-will, and nonviolence of good will, and that violence is therefore intrinsically evil and nonviolence intrinsically good."[22] To the contrary, "Nothing is intrinsically immoral except ill-will and nothing intrinsically good except goodwill."[23]

While pacifism as a formal doctrine was visibly present within the United States and Europe throughout the twentieth century, its influence is not limited to its adherents alone. That is to say, pacifists are not the only ones arguing for pacifism. Shifts in just war theory over the past century have created what Johnson calls "crypto-pacifism"[24] or "functional pacifism."[25] He argues that a new kind of pacifism was created and hidden within just war theory.

In 1983, the United States Conference of Catholic Bishops issued its pastoral letter, "The Challenge of Peace." This document had a remarkable effect on subsequent conversations of just war, for better or worse. Marking

22. Niebuhr, *Moral Man and Immoral Society*, 171.
23. Niebuhr, *Moral Man and Immoral Society*, 170.
24. Johnson, *Ethics and the Use of Force*, 46.
25. Johnson, *Ethics and the Use of Force*, 162.

a significant change in direction for how Roman Catholics think about the ethics of war, the letter first introduced the idea that just war theory demands a "presumption against war."[26] Ten years later, the idea was strengthened to be a "strong presumption against the use of force." This principle was used, then, as an objection to the decision to go to war against Iraq after its invasion of Kuwait—a clear-cut case of a just war by any other measure. It is important to note, however, that this new ethic was not adopted by the bishops' conferences of other countries, but was the "singular invention" of the US Conference.[27] It represents the thinking of one group of people within one religious tradition. Nevertheless, it was powerful and influential.

This position eventually led to what many consider a new requirement of *jus ad bellum* in just war theory: the use of force must be a "last resort" before violence may be justified. This idea has become so commonplace that many people assume it is part of the tradition. There are, however, two important points to be considered with regard to this new principle.

First, it must be recognized as a novelty in the just war theory. That is neither an argument for nor against its value. It is to say that we should recognize that it is a recent innovation that does not reflect a consensus among scholars. It should be critically evaluated, not assumed as normative.

Second, it is essentially an impossible criterion to meet when interpreted literally. When has one reached the "last resort?" Could Churchill have tried one more attempt at diplomacy with Hitler? Did Lincoln need to take one more shot at negotiations with the South before resorting to arms? Should Navy SEALS have first tried to use a Taser on Osama bin Laden before putting two bullets in his head? The fact is that in any potential conflict, someone can always propose one final nonviolent tactic. Walzer addresses the illogic of such a moral condition when he writes that waiting for the last resort "would make war morally impossible. . . . For we can never reach lastness, or we can never know that we have reached it."[28] The word "never" is a bit strong here. We could say that you have only reached the moment of last resort when the gun is to your head and the trigger is being pulled.

This explains Johnson's belief that this "new" just war theory is simply crypto-Pacifism. The conditions to begin hostilities are presented in such a way that they can never be met, despite the claim that they could be. Since

26. The idea was first suggested by Harvard University ethicist Ralph B. Potter Jr. in 1970 (Baer, *Recovering Christian Realism*, 10).

27. Johnson, *Ethics and the Use of Force*, 26. Johnson goes so far as to say that, "[T]he version of just war in *The Challenge of Peace* is starkly different in overall nature and detail from the form, content, method, purpose, and outcome of historical just war tradition" (Johnson, *Ethics and the Use of Force*, 5).

28. Johnson, *Ethics and War*, 95, quoting Walzer.

1983, when the first version of "The Challenge of Peace" was published, there have been no cases when the National Conference of Catholic Bishops felt the standard has been met. One might reasonably ask about those who support a moral condition for a just war that can never be met. In such a case, can the proponent rightly be considered an adherent of just war theory?[29]

It is also important to recognize that a longer delay before engaging an enemy can mean more carnage, not less. Allowing an aggressor nation to fortify its positions only leads to longer conflicts and greater casualties. It can also turn the tides of war, as Union forces discovered at the Battle of Fredericksburg in 1862. General Ambrose Burnside may have delayed for strategic, rather than moral reasons, but the effect was the same, as he lost over twelve thousand men. What could have been a swift victory and an earlier end to the war became one of the Union's most embarrassing losses.

Waiting as long as possible before using violence is often couched in terms of humanitarian concerns. While the carnage of war may be delayed or avoided, that does not always equate to less suffering overall. Waiting out the effects of sanctions may avoid war, but often at the cost of starvation and malnutrition affecting poverty-stricken civilian populations. Consider the hundreds of thousands of children who died in Iraq during the period of economic sanctions, when the child mortality rate in Southern and Central Iraq stood at a staggering 108 per one thousand.[30] If hostilities do happen after a period of "diplomacy," the effects can be far bloodier. In 2017, the world watched this transpire in Syria. A relatively small civil war became a proxy war between Iran and Sunni Arabs, Russia and the United States, Turkey and the Kurds, and ISIS wrought havoc throughout the whole region.

At the same time that some just war theorists have made this move to crypto-pacifism, another notably different shift has taken place in the literature. Rather than the introduction of new requirements, there has been a proposed return to the classic expression of the theory, the dominant understanding prior to Grotius and the Peace of Westphalia.

Scholars like Johnson argue that the current model fails to address realities we face today. Waiting for one sovereign nation to attack another before *jus ad bellum* has been reached may leave us confused about how to respond to intranational catastrophes, like the genocide in Rwanda (when

29. Oliver O'Donovan describes this as "a mere trick." Thus conceived, if "'just war theory' had no purpose but to disprove on a case-by-case basis claims for the justice of particular wars which pacifism had ruled out *a limine*, then it could relate to pacifism like research-assistant to professor, marshalling the detailed evidence in support of the grand hypothesis" (*Just War Revisited*, 8).

30. This statistic reflects the child mortality rate from 1994–1999 (Ali and Shah, "Sanctions and Childhood Mortality," 1851–57).

the world failed to act) or Kosovo (when it did). Is there nothing to be done when an enemy is hiding (or being sheltered) in a non-belligerent country? The US invasion of Afghanistan, execution of Osama bin Laden in Pakistan, and drone strikes in Yemen were not preceded by those nations violating the sovereignty of the United States or its allies. As a result, these remain controversial decisions, especially when viewed by non-Americans who are less keen on granting some kind of American exceptionalism.

To be certain, there has long been tension and disagreement regarding the point at which one nation (or group of nations) may respond with force to perceived injustice within another nation's borders. Pope John Paul II famously argued that intervention is "obligatory where the survival of populations and entire ethnic groups is seriously compromised. This is a duty for nations and the international community."[31] The US Conference of Catholic Bishops cites this approvingly and adds:

> [H]uman life, human rights and the welfare of the human community are at the center of Catholic moral reflection on the social and political order. Geography and political divisions do not alter the fact that we are all one human family, and indifference to the suffering of members of that family is not a moral option. Second, sovereignty and nonintervention into the life of another state have long been sanctioned by Catholic social principles, but have never been seen as absolutes. Therefore, the principles of sovereignty and nonintervention may be overridden by forceful means in exceptional circumstances, notably in the cases of genocide or when whole populations are threatened by aggression or anarchy.[32]

It is no easy task to define "exceptional circumstances." Genocide would probably qualify, if we could agree on a definition. Has the Kim family in North Korea reached that mark, after decades of brutal tyranny? Did South Africa under apartheid? Was the world negligent by not acting decisively in Darfur, where nearly a half million people were killed and three million displaced? Were bombings of Serbia justified?

Governments with a moral compass, along with their citizens, struggle to identify unjust situations where military involvement may be justified. This challenge demands the best of us and is never-ending. Among just war theorists, there is a growing concern that the language that arose in the seventeenth century can be an impediment to these crucial conversations. When just war theory is viewed largely through the lens of sovereign nations

---

31. John Paul II, "Address to the International Conference," 475.

32. "Harvest of Justice," II.E.4.

respecting one another's borders, we are not using and developing the best ethical tools for analyzing highly complex situations. Johnson points out, "These [modern] assumptions, as well as the resulting conceptions of just war, differ significantly from those held by classic just war thinkers."[33]

Modern emphases on universal human rights have led us to recognize that the world bears some moral responsibility for what happens within the borders of other nations. For this reason, some argue that it would be better to return to an earlier conception of just war theory that looks to the "defense of the common good" over the more limiting construct of "self-defense." This is what Johnson favors.

> That is, we have rediscovered, by thinking about human rights, the concept of tyranny; we have rediscovered the idea that sovereignty implies positive obligations to the people over whom one is sovereign. This is a fundamental just war idea, but one which has been obscured by the Westphalian system's focus on sovereignty as tied to territorial borders.[34]

To be certain, this approach opens one up to certain risks, the type for which Europe paid a bloody price when nations went to war with each other to eradicate harmful beliefs "in defense of the common good." The strict rule of self-defense is easier to apply and is less likely to be abused; at the same time, it leaves countless millions at the mercy of tyrants. Classic just war theory allows for more critical dialogue regarding when military action on behalf of these victims is justified, but the imprecise language of the criteria makes us nervous, and rightfully so.

Jus Post Bellum?

In Sikhism, the story is told of a duel between Guru Hargobind (1595–1644) and Painda Khan. After the latter was bested, and lay dying on the ground, the guru held his head in his lap, shielded his eyes from the sun, and said, "Painda, it is time to repeat the *kalmia*."[35] Painda, greatly moved by the compassion of the man who had just dealt him a mortal blow, responded, "Now Guru, your sword has become my *kalmia*."

In addition to the categories of *jus ad bellum* and *jus in bello* discussed previously, there is the proposal for a third: *jus post bellum*, or justice after war. While the name for this consideration is relatively new, it has long

---

33. Johnson, *Ethics and the Use of Force*, 137.
34. Johnson, *Ethics and the Use of Force*, 92.
35. The *kalmia* are the confessions of faith in Islam.

been recognized that a nation's moral responsibility in warfare does not end when the guns fall silent and swords return to their sheaths. John Locke (1632–1704), the "Father of Classical Liberalism," expressed this common conviction: "Let the conqueror have as much justice on his side as could be supposed, he has no right to seize more than the vanquished could forfeit; his life is at the victor's mercy, and his service and goods he may appropriate to make himself reparation but he cannot take the goods of his wife and children."[36]

A war that was engaged for a just cause, fought and won according to strict moral standards, can still be unjust if the victor exceeds certain moral limits after the fighting. There are limits on the spoils of war. A good example would be the Treaty of Versailles, crafted after World War I. The moral, geographic, and financial concessions that Germany was forced to accept are regarded as being far in excess of what was appropriate at the end of the conflict. In and of themselves, they were wrong. They were also significant contributing factors to the rise of Nazism fifteen years later, and World War II after that.

We may also consider the end of the Gulf War, in 1991, when American-led forces brutalized the defeated Iraqi military. The "pounding of retreating troops on the Basra Road in excess of any tactical necessity" did not serve the stated goal of the war, and therefore has been judged by some as an illegitimate act by the allied powers.[37]

Lee explains, "If a war is *post bellum* just, those terms will be a fulfillment of the rightful intentions with which the war began."[38] If Augustine was right that the purpose of war is to create peace, then a war that perpetuates or escalates future violence—regardless of its just cause and conduct—is unjust.

The Iraq War, conducted under the leadership of George W. Bush, may be an example of this. While this war has been considered by many people as a terrible mistake, this is often due more to what happened after the major military operations, rather than the decision to go to war itself (although plenty of people objected to this as well).

Saddam Hussein had invaded Kuwait in 1991, and had been justly expelled during the presidency of George H. W. Bush. That conflict had ended with a ceasefire, the conditions of which were repeatedly violated by the Iraqi dictator for twelve years. The continued sanctions resulted in hundreds of thousands of deaths, as mentioned above, and failed to contain

36. Locke, *Second Treatise of Government*, 183.

37. O'Donovan, *Just War Revisited*, 52.

38. Lee, *Ethics and War*, 287.

the despot's ambitions. In addition, the sincere belief that Iraq was developing chemical and nuclear weapons—shared universally and encouraged by Hussein himself—added to the urgency some felt to intervene.

While the initial invasion was a considerable success, the United States and its allies became bogged down in Iraq, failing miserably. The resulting civil war, which ravaged the country and played a role in the rise of ISIS in 2015, was clearly not a case of war bringing peace. It is worth pondering, however, how we would judge this war if it had succeeded in deposing Hussein and creating a stable Iraq. Chances are good that we would commend George W. Bush for his decision to eliminate the "Butcher of Baghdad" and create a democracy in the Middle East. Unfortunately, the *post bellum* reality of Iraq turned out to be quite different than what was expected. This, I believe, should be understood as the ethical failing of the Iraq War, rather than a simple condemnation of the decision to take up arms a second time against a brutal regime.

If violence is undertaken to serve the public good, then one is morally responsible for achieving that end. If that end cannot be achieved, then violence must be rejected.[39]

It is important to note that *jus post bellum* is not a generally accepted category of just war theory. There are those who believe that it is simply subsumed under *jus ad bellum*. That is to say, the criteria for entering war include responsibility for a just peace. Johnson argues, "Sometimes this is described as the problem of *jus post bellum*, though in my own judgment it is already implied in the classic just war conception that the use of armed force is justified only when it aims at restoring or establishing peace."[40]

I believe that Johnson is correct, but at the same time it is also helpful to have an additional classification for ethical consideration of complex events like war. It may be redundant, but this redundancy may be helpful.

39. In fairness to the younger President Bush, his intentions were to create a peaceful and stable Iraq. However, this does not remove all moral culpability for failing to do so.

40. Johnson, *Ethics and the Use of Force*, 166.

PART FOUR

Civilian Self-Defense
When to Fight

Wait until the situation compels you to fight when you have no desire to do so.

—MARTIN LUTHER

Generally speaking, discussing the ethics of just war theory may be interesting, but far removed from our everyday lives. Most of us do not make decisions about when our nations go to war or how to conduct combat missions. Of course, we should educate ourselves about these issues and communicate our beliefs to our government and other voters. Moreover, some readers may find themselves in combat someday; their ethical decision-making will be aided by having considered moral arguments related to just war theory. For most readers, however, this theory remains quite distant from our daily lives of work, play, and family.

Much closer to home are questions regarding acts of violence in our own communities—situations of civilian self-defense. How should I respond if someone physically threatens me? Should I intervene if I encounter someone else being assaulted? Certainly there are important legal considerations, regarding what I am permitted to do. However, for those who strive to live by a code of ethics, there are also questions about what I should do. Here we find that eternal ethical dilemma that men and women face from time to time: "*Should* I punch that person in the mouth?" To be sure, there are legal concerns (e.g., "Will I go to jail or be sued if I do?"), as well as practical considerations (e.g., "*Can* I hit him? Will that stop him? Will I just get my own ass kicked?"). This book is primarily concerned with the ethics of violence. While there is a great deal of overlap between the law and morality, they are not the same thing. Some actions are legal but may still be immoral.

Ethical questions related to civilian self-defense are important and practical. When should I fight? How ought I to fight? Can I ever throw the first punch? When should I intervene on another's behalf? Do I have a moral duty to avoid violence whenever possible? Is stabbing someone in the neck ever morally justifiable?

These are important questions for people to ask themselves. When a violent situation unfolds, there is little time for ethical rumination. Having worked through your own moral convictions beforehand is essential to acting in good conscience when the ugliness of life unfolds. You and I may not agree on everything related to the ethics of violence, but we should both know where we stand before anything hits the fan. This prevents poor decision-making in the moment. Just as an athlete, soldier, or firefighter must train assiduously in order to respond well in the moment, so the same is true for all of us when it comes to ethics. Unfortunately, this is very rarely realized, let alone practiced (even among those who study ethics for a living).

When it comes to the tricky matter of the ethics of civilian violence, just war theory provides a valuable resource to think through the moral dimensions of violence in which we may find ourselves. Whether a decision must be reached in an instant, or there is time to mull over a proper response, a clear set of moral guidelines is of tremendous importance and help. The use of just war theory's categories can help one think more clearly about moral choices.[41] Moreover, when the consequences of our decisions can include lawsuits, arrest, our mental and physical health, or our very lives, not to mention the lives and well-being of others, clear thinking is essential.

To be sure, not all principles of just war theory carry over into civilian encounters with violence. Soldiers are in the business of killing; we civilians are very rarely faced with situations that require such a level of force. Civilians are generally expected to end hostilities against a threat short of killing someone; soldiers much less so. Civilians are usually wise to flee from

41. Scholars who advocate for reductive individualism (e.g., Walzer and Frowe) argue that the right of nations to use force is essentially no different than the right of individuals. Rather than talking about the rights of individuals being extended to governments, I am reversing this perspective here. I want to ask how just war theory can shed light on the ethics of individual self-defense.

violence, while military and law enforcement personnel do not have that luxury—quite the opposite in most cases. Lastly, civilians generally do not have to think about collateral damage if we end up in a scrap. Those who fire missiles and automatic weapons have this additional moral obligation. Nevertheless, thinking in terms of when I should engage in violence (*jus ad bellum*) and how I should conduct myself in the midst of violence (*jus in bello*) is a helpful way to begin.

Life presents us with unanticipated moral challenges, and can do so quite suddenly. If some nasty bigot shoves my young son in a restaurant, am I morally justified in punching him? If so, how many times? Can I punch him in the throat? I believe that using just war theory as a model can be tremendously useful. This is what we will consider in the following two chapters.

CHAPTER 7

When to Fight

Jus ad bellum

Self-defence is Nature's eldest law.

—JOHN DRYDEN

The reader will recall that *jus ad bellum* deals with the moral permissibility of entering into war. While the comparison is not perfect, it does help us to consider ethical questions related to whether or not we should enter into violent encounters within a civilian context.

Proper Authority and Just Cause

Just war theory begins, as we have seen, with the important principle that only a "proper authority" may enter into war. Civilians do not have the legal or moral authority to engage in war of their own accord. If they are given authorization by legitimate authorities, after volunteering or being drafted into military service, then they may go and fight. However, they must explicitly be granted that permission and right by the government.

The same ethical construct holds true when it comes to the context of civilian violence. To put it simply, when considering an act of violence against my neighbor, I must consider whether I have legal authority to do so. Does my government grant me permission to use physical force in this situation? If not, then I may not do so.

In the same way that an officer, soldier, or pilot may kill an enemy *only* when acting in accordance with the government's directive, and within the parameters of recognized rules of war, so the civilian should only use violence within a context and in a manner permitted by the government. Thus, before you or I engage in the use of physical force against another human being in our community, we should consider the following question: "Do I have legal authority to do so?"

Civilians generally do not have authority to use violence; we have given up this right to our nations' military and law enforcement bodies. However, the government extends temporary authority in particular situations when an individual may act on the basis of a just cause. For example, I may use violence if a person starts running amok in the mall, stabbing people at will. However, once that assault has ended, I am no longer permitted to use violence. Thus, it is essential to know the law—when individual citizens are permitted to use violence, and when they are not.

In my own state of Pennsylvania, the law regarding self-defense reads: "The use of force upon or toward another person is justifiable when the actor believes that such force is immediately necessary for the purpose of protecting himself against the use of unlawful force by such other person on the present occasion" (Pa.C.S. § 505). In cases such as these, I am legally permitted to use force against another person.

When I was twenty-one years old, I had a disagreement with a stranger in the parking garage of the Trump Taj Mahal in Atlantic City.[1] The other gentleman took exception to my stance on the subject under discussion and jumped out of his car with a baseball bat. He continued expressing his opinion of my point of view and of me, and then proceeded to rush at me. In that case, self-defense would likely have been legally justified. I would have had proper authority to act because of a just cause that presented itself. (As we will see later, when we return to this story, it did not mean that I was morally good-to-go, completely justified in charging back with the intent to sweep him off his feet and drive the back of his skull into the pavement. Spoiler alert: I didn't.)

Pennsylvania state law (§ 506) also permits me to use force "for the protection of other persons" when the safety of another is at stake, as spelled out in § 505, quoted above. Thus, if I come across some ruffian violently shoving an elderly man on the street, and I were to intervene, I could use force to stop him from injuring the other man.

---

1. This incident was in New Jersey, not Pennsylvania, but the laws are comparable for the sake of this example.

Nevertheless, the fact that I may have legal authority to act with physical force in both of these cases does not mean that it is the morally right thing to do. It also does not mean that I can engage in any act of physical force I choose to use. The case in Atlantic City would permit more force, as the danger from the man wielding the bat (who was high on drugs [did I mention that earlier?]) was far greater than someone shoving another person. In both of these situations, all that may be determined is that I would have "proper authority" to act based on a "just cause," as granted to me by my government. However, there are still other concerns we need to consider.

It is important to understand that the difference between legal and illegal use of force is murky and nuanced. There is a reason that lawmakers keep adding amendments and qualifications to laws, and that lawyers make many millions of dollars debating these laws and their applications, as they prosecute and defend people who are caught up in violent acts.

One very important consideration to remember is that different countries, and different states within some countries, have different laws. As we saw in the previous section, it is not always easy to determine what a "just cause" for fighting is. Whether or not you have legal grounds to kick someone in the crotch can vary depending on your location. As discussed above, if that person is about to hit you in the head with a metal pipe without provocation, and you cannot get away from the situation, then you are generally justified in responding with a significant level of force. Likewise, if he is about to hit some other innocent bystander, you can do the same in defense of the other. However, in many places, if you have the opportunity to retreat, you *must* attempt to do so.

If a three-hundred-pound man with a bum leg is hobbling toward me, threatening to do me grievous bodily harm when he gets his hands on me, I may have a legal obligation to flee if I can. This "duty to retreat" means I may not have the "proper authority" to use violence. Back in 1992, when I was visiting Atlantic City and faced the man charging at me with the baseball bat, it was not only prudent for me to turn and run (which I did), but it was also legally required. I was able to retreat; therefore, I was required to do so by New Jersey state law.

If you live in a place where the "castle doctrine" is law, then you may stand and fight if the threat exists in your home. If a person intent on doing you harm is walking through your front door, you are not legally obligated to try to run out your back door. You are permitted to stand and defend your "castle."

If your state has a "stand your ground" law, then you have the right to stand and defend yourself with physical force if you are in any location where you have a lawful right to be. In Pennsylvania, if I am standing outside the mall—waiting for my wife to finish shopping, again—I am in such a location. If someone approaches me and threatens to smash my face in, I have no legal duty to retreat. I can stand my ground. If the other person provokes a fight, and I need to defend myself, I may do so.

In all of these situations, the law does not grant me the authority to respond with any level of force I choose. If an irate shopper in the grocery store shoves me, I cannot shoot her. I can only respond with lethal force if I fear severe bodily injury or death. In Pennsylvania, it is difficult to make that claim if the aggressor is unarmed; in Florida, the person need not be armed to justify a lethal act of self-defense.[2]

While these few paragraphs are obviously not an authoritative legal guidebook, they illustrate the necessity of knowing one's local laws. If people want to know if they have "proper authority" to engage in physical violence in a particular situation, they need to know what the law says. They need to understand what their government considers "just cause." Moreover, one should remember that the details of any given situation make these circumstances infinitely varied and difficult to judge.

Before we continue, the reader should again note that there is a difference between a legal right to use violence and the morality of that act. If we are using just war theory as a model for civilian self-defense, having legal authority and just cause to use force is only part of the moral equation. As cited in the previous chapter, Hugo Grotius (the seventeenth-century theological ethicist) and Thomas Aquinas (the thirteenth-century theologian) wrote about the ethics of facing an unjust aggressor: "Even under such circumstances the one who is attacked ought to prefer to do anything possible to frighten away or weaken the assailant, rather than cause his death."[3]

Strike first, strike hard?

In just war theory, one country does not need to be attacked first for there to be just cause to defend itself through force of arms. Violence that is "imminent, but not actual" is sufficient justification for a nation to claim self-defense. As discussed above, Israel's preemptive attack on Egypt in 1967 is generally regarded as meeting this requirement.

The same is true with individual self-defense. While your mother, father, or principal may have told you never to throw the first punch, the law does not demand such a standard. Violence that is imminent may be

---

2. As one particularly well-known example, see the Trayvon Martin case.
3. As in Johnson, *Ethics and the Use of Force*, 81.

sufficient to allow us to use violence to defend ourselves. In such a case, a person has just cause to initiate physical force.

My friend who works in loss prevention at a major retail store had an interesting encounter several years back. A large, muscular man walked into his store and headed to the hardware section. He picked up a maul,[4] slung it over his shoulder, and walked out the door. My friend, short and stocky and with considerable martial arts background—both theoretical and applied—approached him in the parking lot. He calmly explained that the man and the merchandise needed to return to the store.

Unfortunately, the thief declined the polite invitation and more words were spoken. Finally, the brawny shoplifter yelled, "You want this? I'll give it to you! But you're not going to like it when I give it to you!" He then put two hands on the handle and drew it back as if to swing. My friend could not tell if this was a bluff; the man had not started to swing the maul forward, but he had pulled it back as if to initiate an attack. This was obviously a very dangerous situation—a life-threatening situation. Standing there and talking, or trying to retreat at that point, would not remove my friend from danger. Trying either to block or evade such an attack would be extremely difficult. Therefore, before any forward swing, he stepped in, checked the handle of the maul with his left hand, and punched the man square in the face with his right. The man absent-mindedly let go of his weapon as he stumbled back. As he then looked up, he saw my friend standing there holding the maul with one hand looking back at him. The disarmed thief remarked, "I guess you take your job seriously." "I do," was the response. And they both headed back into the store.

We should remember, however, that not every threat of violence meets the standard of being imminent. A few years ago I exchanged words with two young men who were in a car, slowly driving down the street. The fellow in the passenger seat made a threatening remark, something to the effect of how he was going to come over and cram my eyeglasses down my throat. However, he made no move to exit his car, which was now driving slowly away from where I was. At that point, I would obviously have been acting without just cause, and without legitimate authority, if I ran over and punched the guy in the face through his open car window.

The line between preemptive self-defense and starting a fight is not always clear. Not too long ago, I was on my way to the gas station when another vehicle failed to stop at a red light and barely avoided t-boning me. We both hit our brakes and looked at each other. I saw that his negligence was

4. For those unfamiliar with this tool, imagine an axe handle with a head that is ½ axe, ½ sledgehammer.

due to him talking on his phone, and so I proceeded to yell and gesticulate at him from within my car. As I went on my way, he followed me to the gas station and pulled his truck in sideways in front of my car at the pump, blocking my exit. We both exited our vehicles and he approached me, yelling. This struck me as odd, as he had clearly been at fault. However, he thought I had given him a particular universal hand gesture from my car, which he could not countenance. (For the record, I had not. Honestly!) He came over to me, while I loudly declared (for the benefit of potential witnesses) that I did not want any trouble. We had a heated discussion about the events that had just transpired, and he was determined to put me in my place. He even began poking his finger into my chest.

In that case, would I have been legally justified in dropping him with a first punch to his overactive mandible? Probably. However, for all of his bravado, I sensed (correctly, as is it turned out) that he did not really want to fight. He wanted to express his frustration with me. If in the midst of that face-to-face conversation, however, he had suddenly become quiet and looked at the ground, then I would have been more likely to throw that first punch. His actions would have been an indicator that an attack was on the verge of happening. (Of course, the police and district attorney may not have seen it that way—depending on how much they know about interpersonal violence.)

Getting inside others' heads to know their intent is impossible. The law allows us to make reasonable inferences, but there is no clear line to draw on the subject. With regard to warfare, Michael Walzer argues that

> The line between legitimate and illegitimate first strikes is not going to be drawn at the point of imminent attack but at the point of sufficient threat. That phrase is necessarily vague. I mean it to cover three things: a manifest intent to injure, a degree of active preparation that makes that intent a positive danger, and a general situation in which waiting, or doing anything other than fighting, greatly magnifies the risk.[5]

A legal right to use violence, however, is different than a moral right to do so. There are quite a number of moral arguments that have been made against ever striking first. Grotius wrote, "[T]o pretend to have a Right to injure another, merely from a Possibility that he may injure me, is repugnant to all the Justice in the World: For such is the condition of present Life, that we can never be in perfect Security."[6] Vitoria also expressed a strong moral

5. Walzer, *Just and Unjust Wars*, 81.
6. Grotius, *On the Law of War and Peace*, 417. As in Lee, *Ethics and War*, 78.

objection to lethal first strikes. "It is quite unacceptable that a person should be killed for a sin he has yet to commit."[7]

With regard to civilian self-defense, this is certainly a tricky matter. However, the moral dilemma receives some clarification by considering the contributions made by a particular society from a small island in East Asia: the people of Okinawa. This culture has taught both the practice and the ethics of civilian self-defense for at least 150 years, and their wisdom is certainly of considerable help to us today.

There is no first attack?

One of the most famous moral principles in karate—the indigenous martial art of Okinawa—is the rule *Karate ni sente nashi* ("In karate there is no first attack"). It was Gichin Funakoshi (1868–1957), the father of modern karate, who made this statute so well-known. He gave it a place of prominence in his *Niji Kun* ("Twelve Precepts"), a moral code that is proudly displayed in thousands of karate schools around the world today. He even stated that it expresses "the essence of karate-do."[8]

Karate students recite this principle every day. They are taught that this is the reason that their *kata* (or forms) always begin with a block, and that this is a discipline not about fighting but purely for self-defense. It is not surprising, then, that many people believe that there are no preemptive strikes in this fighting style and the philosophy that undergirds it. However, that turns out to be wrong.

During the golden age of karate (in the early twentieth century), at the same time that Funakoshi was teaching this principle, other karate patriarchs were teaching something quite different: they advised their pupils to hit the other guy first. Just as Israel knew in 1967, and my friend knew in the store parking lot, these karate teachers also realized that waiting for an attack to be launched before striking back makes it much more likely that you will die.

Choki Motobu (1870–1944), admittedly something of a ruffian, wrote in his *Watashi no Karate-jutsu* ("My karate-jutsu") in 1932,

> But when a situation can't be helped, in other words, when, even though one tries to avoid trouble, one can't; when an enemy is

---

7. Vitoria, *Vitoria: Political Writings*, 316. As in Lee, *Ethics and War*, 80.

8. *Karate no Hanashi*, 65. As in Tankosich, "Karate ni Sente Nashi." Tankosich also quotes famous teachers Shoshin Nagamine ("this phrase . . . embodies the essence of Okinawan karate") and Masatoshi Nakayama ("it is not an exaggeration to say that it is these words that succinctly and fully express the spirit of karate-do").

serious about doing one harm, one must fiercely stand and fight. When one does fight, taking control of the enemy is crucial, and one must take that control with one's first move. Thus, in a fight one must attack first. It is very important to remember this.[9]

Likewise, Kenwa Mabuni (1889–1952), who enjoyed a much better reputation, wrote the following: "When faced with someone who disrupts the peace or who will do one harm, one is as a warrior gone to battle, and so it only stands to reason that one should get the jump on the enemy and preempt his use of violence. Such action in no way goes against the precept of *sente nashi*."[10] What Motobu and Mabuni knew, and tried to convey to their students, was that waiting for someone to "throw the first punch" is not smart. It is important to note that they were not talking about low-stake brawls, or "dust-ups," between guys looking for bragging rights. They had in mind situations that could be matters of life or death. In such contexts, the bravado of saying "Go ahead, take the first shot" could mean you get hit with a truncheon, or stabbed with a knife, and left for dead on the side of the road.

Japanese teachers of martial arts, beyond karate, have long taught the strategy of *sensen no sen*. Unlike *go no sen* (blocking and counter-striking) and *sen no sen* (intercepting an incoming strike by moving faster to the target), the principle of *sensen no sen* means preempting the opponent's movement entirely by perceiving his intention.[11] Here, you do not wait for the opponent to pull back his hand, but strike in the moment between his intention and his first physical movement. This idea, which is often taught by the same people teaching "no first strike in karate," appears on the face of it to be quite at odds with Funakoshi's principle.

This is not the case, however. Mabuni explained the compatibility of *sente nashi* (no first strike) and *sensen no sen* (strike prior to prior). Here is the context of his statement quoted above:

> There is a precept "*karate ni sente nashi*." Properly understood, this indicates a mental attitude of not being eager or inclined to fight. It is the teaching that just because one has trained in karate does not mean that one can rashly strike or kick others . . .
>
> When faced with someone who disrupts the peace or who will do one harm, one is as a warrior gone to battle, and so it

9. Tankosich, "Karate ni Sente Nashi," 21.

10. Tankosich, "Karate ni Sente Nashi," 23.

11. Notice that the word *sen* (先) is the same as in "karate has no *sen-te*," (先手; "first hand"/"strike"). Thus, you find one principle of no first ("prior") strike and another which encourages acting "prior" to the initiation of a first strike.

only stands to reason that one should get the jump on the enemy and preempt his use of violence. Such action in no way goes against the precept of *sente nashi*.

[There] is a mistaken understanding found among some karate practitioners. It is a view that does not see *sente nashi* as an attitude, but rather as a literal, behavioral rule to be rigidly followed. As noted above, when absolutely necessary, when one is already facing a battle, it is an accepted truth of strategy that one should try to take *sensen no sen* and forestall the enemy's actions.

In conclusion, the expression *karate ni sente nashi* should be properly understood to mean that a person who practices karate must never take a bellicose attitude, looking to cause an incident; he or she should always have the virtues of calmness, prudence and humility in dealing with others.[12]

Without using the vocabulary of ethical theory, Mabuni pointed out the difference between deontology and virtue ethics. We in the West are quite familiar with absolute moral principles and rules (e.g., the Ten Commandments, the Golden Rule, Kant's Categorical Imperative). We use them a lot in our moral reasoning. Moreover, some people (including this author) are more inclined toward a bit of legalism, preferring strict non-negotiable rules. Thus, many karate students have come across Funakoshi's prohibition on a "first strike" and interpret it as an absolute precept—never throw the first punch. However, East Asian cultures—with Okinawa as no exception—operate much more in the realm of virtue ethics. Rather than hard and fast rules, ethics often take the form of describing and modeling character traits. We can see, then, that Funakoshi was describing the kind of person that karate practitioners should strive to be—one who is not "eager or inclined to fight." He was describing a virtue. Many of us, with our love of absolute moral rules, are inclined to take this precept and make it a fixed truth: "Never attack first!"

Motobu noticed people in his own context doing this and recognized the foolhardiness of such an ethic. From a utilitarian standpoint, following such a rule can get you killed. In his typically iconoclastic way, he turned the principle upside down to make an important point. "When one does fight, taking control of the enemy is crucial, and one must take that control with one's first move. Thus, in a fight one *must* attack first. It is very important to remember this."[13]

12. Tankosich, "Karate ni Sente Nashi," 23.

13. Tankosich, "Karate ni Sente Nashi," 21 (emphasis added).

The ethic that governs Okinawan karate, then, is one that teaches practitioners to shun violence, to avoid fights, and to be a lover of peace. However, when another person is determined to cause you serious bodily injury or death, your best chance at survival involves seizing the initiative at the earliest possible moment—even before your enemy's intent manifests itself in action.

A final example of this may help, both to illustrate the ethic in action and also its limitations. Choki Motobu, the thuggish Okinawan karate teacher discussed above, was once challenged to a fight by a former student. The young man had burst into a party where Motobu was present, insisting on a life-and-death match with knives. He was adamant that the fight take place, stabbing a knife into Motobu's table. The teacher's resolute insistence that he would not fight with a knife fell on deaf ears, as the student only insisted more that they settle the issue. Finally, Motobu told him, "I will take you up on your offer, but we should not fight in the house." As the student grabbed his knife and headed toward the door, Motobu followed closely behind and kicked him in the back, "shattering his backbone."[14]

In this case, Motobu certainly lived out his principle that "in a fight one must attack first." There was clear intent, opportunity, and ability on the part of his adversary, and so we may grant that Motobu acted in self-defense with a preemptive attack. Personally, if someone were determined to carve me up with a knife, I would certainly be willing to kick him in the back to keep myself safe. I am also pretty sure that my wife and kids back home would not object. At the same time, in Motobu's case, one wonders if the time necessary for both men to walk out the door could have allowed for a less vicious attack—something other than paralyzing the man. Could he have fled? Was there something nearby with which he could have hit him over the head instead? Could he have used a less devastating strike?

The reality is, of course, that we do not know. And hindsight is always twenty-twenty. However, this returns us to Funakoshi's famous dictum. While dangerous situations may present themselves, one should be a lover of peace; never eager to start violence, yet able to end it. The two must exist together, balancing one another so that peace may be preserved whenever possible, and unavoidable violence may be curbed as quickly as possible.

Recovery of Something Wrongfully Taken

In classical just war theory, "recovery of something wrongfully taken" was considered a just cause for going to war. Can the same apply to individuals

14. As in Tankosich, "Karate ni Sente Nashi," 22.

in civil society today? Can you use force against another person if she steals your possessions? Is it acceptable to use force on behalf of another who has had something stolen?

In 2013, brothers Andrew and Joel Leach of Chicago were out walking one evening when they witnessed a woman being assaulted and robbed. Robert Henderson had bitten the woman and stolen her cell phone. The two brothers proceeded to chase him down. Henderson stopped to face them, whipped out a knife, and asked, "Do you guys want to get cut?" At that point, one of the brothers pulled his own knife and replied, "Mine's bigger than yours." Henderson took off running again.

Eventually the brothers caught the thief and told him, "Look, all we want is her property." Henderson told them where he had dropped it, and was eventually taken into custody by the police. While the article does not detail any specifics of force used by Andrew or Joel, the threat of cutting or stabbing Robert with a larger knife meant that violence could easily have been in play.

As discussed above, when considering just cause for civilian use of violence, we must ask what legitimate authority is granted by the government. If I steal your pen, you cannot walk up and punch me in the face. Whether it is a fitting punishment in your mind is irrelevant. You can, however, walk up and attempt to take it back. The line that cannot be crossed when attempting to recover something wrongfully taken is in your state's existing laws. You cannot break a law to regain your property. For example, you cannot punch someone unconscious so you can retrieve the wallet he just picked from your pocket. Likewise, you cannot walk into a thief's home to retrieve your possessions. (If they are on the front porch, however, going that far may be acceptable.) If the only way to recover your property involves violating a law, then you are legally and morally required to leave it to the proper authorities.

Real life, however, is usually a little less cut-and-dried than that. If someone snatches your beloved Phillies cap and puts it on his own head, you are legally permitted to try and snatch it back. You can't break his nose to facilitate its return (or punish the brute). However, if you reach for your hat on his head, you know very well that he is likely to push you away. The fact that he has taken your hat means that he already believes himself to be physically superior in this situation. The repeated attempt to reclaim your hat is likely to escalate into violence. Even if you are completely in compliance with the law, repeating that you just want your property back as you try to regain the hat, you know very well that the "bad guy" is likely to escalate the situation to the point where self-defense may be necessary, or at least permitted. This may in fact be either person's goal, to end up in a fight.

Thus, it is possible to adhere to the law in a way that you know will encourage the other person to escalate the force in the situation. Many jerks need only a little impetus to throw a punch, against which you may defend yourself. From a legal standpoint, you may be within your rights. The morality is another question.

I would suggest two good reasons that a person may attempt to recover stolen property in a manner in which doing so may lead to violence: 1) the value of the stolen item may be high enough that a person may want to risk injury to reclaim it; 2) one believes that acting in this case is required for the exercise of justice.

There are items that we possess that are of such monetary or symbolic value (or both) that we would risk our safety to try and retrieve them. For example, I often take my wedding ring off while working out in the gym. If someone grabbed it and ran, I would definitely take off after him and attempt to get it back, even though I know that when I catch up with the thief, violence could possibly result (prompted by the thief, of course). In such cases, a cost-benefit analysis is an appropriate consideration before giving chase. How valuable is the item? Is it replaceable? How dangerous is the other person? If a twelve-year-old girl snatches my wedding ring, I will run her down and peacefully re-obtain my property. If an adult who may be armed grabs my wallet in an unfamiliar city, I would not give chase. Getting stabbed in an alley trying to retrieve things that can be replaced is foolish. It is also being a bad husband and father.

If a playground bully keeps stealing the other kids' Star Wars action figures and is able to get away with it, this behavior is likely to continue and even be reinforced. Sometimes it is necessary for one person to stand up and demand the bully give it back. Whether one's own toys were in the mix or not does not necessarily matter. Sometimes one must take a stand for what is right. However, as any kid who spent time on a playground knows, trying to retrieve a coveted item from a bully may result in a black eye. For adults, the stakes can be much higher. Rarely, however, do we find ourselves in a situation where we need to take a stand, at the risk to our own safety, to retrieve a stolen item for the sake of justice. If such a situation does occur, where the effort is perceived to be warranted, there may be reason to act. However, we must be sure that we are honest with our intentions. We cannot condone any type of vigilantism where we simply want to punish those who do us wrong.

The example of the Leach brothers falls into this type of ambiguity. The two brothers decided to come to the aid of a woman whose property was wrongfully taken. They did not assault the man, but were more than prepared to defend themselves in their lawful attempt to reclaim her property.

Whether this was a noble pursuit of justice, or a reckless pursuit of glory, is impossible to gauge in the minds of others. It is difficult enough to discern it in our own motivations.

Punishment of evildoers

The desire to punish those who have done us, or others, some wrong is quite powerful. Being able to mete out retribution quickly and personally appeals to many of us at times, and there is certainly something attractive about being the agent of justice. It appeals to our sense of fairness, courage, and nobility. It also appeals to our self-righteousness and revelry in power at times. Regardless of the motivations, however, it is almost always inappropriate to carry out oneself.

Classic just war theory permitted a nation to go to war against another in order to punish evildoers. While controversial, it still required the one carrying out the punishment to have the proper authority for doing so. In societies like ours, private citizens are never given the authority to punish one another. That authority does not lie with the police either, but solely with the courts. You and I have no authority to punish evildoers, and so any act of violence which seeks that end is *prima facie* immoral. In the seventeenth century, Grotius wrote, "In a private war [such as individual self-defense] we have only a Regard to our own Defense, but the supreme Powers have not only a Right of Self-Defense, but of revenging and punishing Injuries."[15]

Thus, any justification for violence that is based on the idea that a person needs to be taught a lesson is not morally defensible. That "lesson" may be intended as punishment for some misdeed, or for the sake of deterrence, but it does not matter. Civilians are not given authority to punish one another for their crimes.[16]

Although the role of vigilante is an attractive one, especially to teenage boys (of any age!), it must be rejected. We understand the appeal of

15. Grotius, *On the Law of War and Peace*, 416. As in Lee, *Ethics and War*, 57.

16. There are meaningful objections to this claim that are worthy of consideration, but beyond the scope of this introduction. For example, a scenario is suggested where Victim is being raped by Aggressor, who is much larger and more powerful, such that Victim will not be able to stop him. Victim can, however, break Aggressor's wrist, even though this will not stop the rape. Most people would grant Victim's right to do so. Is such an act, then, not punitive? The problem I have with this argument, and many like it, is that it suggests foreknowledge that is impossible. Victim has the right to fight back in self-defense, and any action Victim takes could conceivably stop the attack at any time. Differentiating an act as either punishment or self-defense in such a case is impossible.

the utilitarian argument for punishing others ourselves: "He won't do that again!" It is not really surprising that so many people love Batman and Frank Castle. After all, it is not hard to imagine good consequences as a result of someone "taking the law into his own hands." However, doing so is a clear example of "making oneself an exception to the rule." If it is acceptable for me to do it, it must be acceptable for others as well. Obviously, we cannot desire a society where anyone could make herself an exception to the rules, to be above the law, whenever she felt a strong desire to do so. While you may have absolute confidence in yourself, and maybe your close friends, take a look at your fellow citizens; for example, the next time you visit the Department of Motor Vehicles. If it is acceptable for you to play the role of vigilante, it is acceptable for all of them as well.

As discussed in chapter 3, one of the noblest "vigilantes" (in my opinion) was Dietrich Bonhoeffer (1906–1945). This German pastor and seminary professor became involved in an assassination attempt on Adolf Hitler during World War II. If ever there was a good cause, a utilitarian calculation designed to bring about a greater good, it was an attempt to kill Hitler. Bonhoeffer and his friends failed, and he was executed in Flossenbürg concentration camp shortly before the end of the war. However, would he have achieved a greater good for Germany and the world if he and his cohorts had succeeded?

As it turned out, the suicide of Hitler achieved a break with the Third Reich for Germany in a way that an assassinated Hitler would not have. Again, a murdered Hitler may have been replaced by new Nazi leadership which was just as bad, or more skilled at warfare, or which may have negotiated a peace settlement with the Allies. The unconditional surrender of Germany and complete break with Nazism may not have happened if Bonhoeffer's Operation Valkyrie had been successful. As it turns out, this was a far better end than Bonhoeffer could have created. Recall that the biggest limitation with utilitarianism is that we can never know all the consequences that will follow from our actions.

Arguments for vigilantism are usually based on Act Utilitarianism. Are there not cases where the greatest good may be served by breaking the rules? Of course! However, one must remember that any such act sets a precedent. When an act of vigilantism is perceived to create a greater good—especially in those cases!—this emboldens others to anoint themselves as being above the law in other situations. This breakdown in respect for the law, along with the destructive results of such actions, make for an even stronger utilitarian argument *against* such acts. Meting out punishment must remain in the hands of appropriate authorities, and them alone.

While vigilantism must be rejected, it is not difficult for some people to see a way around this. It is possible to provoke someone to violence so that self-defense can be used. The legal escalation of a situation, where stronger words and posturing may push the other person to act first, can be a way around this. While this may sound unethical—the discovery of an ethical loophole—it is certainly attractive in some cases.

If someone comes up and spits in your face, is it really best to offer no response? If someone dumps a milkshake on your mother's head, and walks away laughing, what moral recourse is available? We can imagine innumerable circumstances where someone does something horribly offensive—even illegal—but without creating a situation in which you fear for your own safety, and there are no police around. What then?

There are many reasons to avoid vengeance. In a situation where you are genuinely wronged, but not in any physical danger, Christianity and Hinduism provide some sage advice, as discussed in earlier chapters. The Sermon on the Mount was where Jesus taught his disciples to turn the other cheek when slapped, and suffer many other abuses rather than resort to violence. Gandhi taught us, "The weak can never forgive. Forgiveness is the attribute of the strong." To walk away from a provocation may feel like weakness, but it may be the epitome of strength. Likewise, Saint Peter taught this: "Do not repay evil with evil or insult with insult. On the contrary, repay evil with blessing, because to this you were called so that you may inherit a blessing."[17]

There are some situations, however, where forcing the hand of a criminal appears to be morally right, or at least permissible. Leo Gaje, the controversial teacher of Pekiti Tirsia,[18] took this approach when he moved to New York City. "[H]e used to ride the subways late at night with money hanging out of his pickets, looking half-asleep in hopes that someone would attempt to mug him so he could practice his martial arts."[19] Even with noble intentions, this raises all kinds of concerns. From a deontological standpoint, initiating violence is not permitted, and this runs very close to "entrapment." From a utilitarian standpoint, it is certainly easier to justify deterring street crime in this way. After all, people often need a good reason to stop engaging in bad behavior that otherwise benefits them. Moreover, the thief's next victim may have otherwise faced a worse crime, and may not have been in

---

17. 1 Pet 3:9. I often wonder if Gichin Funakoshi had something similar in mind when he wrote, "One thing I often say to my young pupils they find confusing. 'You must,' I tell them,' become not strong but weak'" (*Karate-Do*, 114).

18. Pekiti Tirsia is a brutally effective martial art from the Philippines.

19. "Man Who Never Was," 28–29.

a position to defend herself. An imperfect measure of justice is better than none.

However, if we are counting possible consequences, we must also consider other likely results of escalating situations to the point of violence: you could get beat up, which hurts and further emboldens the other person; you could get stabbed or shot; win or lose, you may have acted illegally and can now be arrested and/or sued; you might win, but then the perpetrator goes home and takes it out on his daughter, giving her a black eye before passing out drunk. Not all possible consequences can be foreseen, but we can recognize some that have a significant likelihood of playing out.

There is one other consequence to discuss when we allow ourselves to suffer silently—the effect on those around us. Allowing oneself to suffer indignity can have a profound influence on those around you. It signals very clearly to others who is more vicious and who is more virtuous. Gandhi and King made great use of the media, when they and their followers allowed themselves to be victimized by the authorities. People around the world read about them in their newspapers, and the support for their respective movements grew. When you choose to fight back, people perceive two combatants. When you do not, it is much easier to see who is in the wrong.

In 2016, a supporter of one political candidate for the presidency of the United States was at a rally in San Jose, California, when she was assaulted and pelted with eggs. She could have fought back, pushed the people around her, and returned the profanity that was hurled at her. She did not, however, respond in that way. She stood there passively and forced a smile. When this made the news, you can guess who benefited the most, her candidate or the one supported by the angry mob?[20]

At the same time, one should remember that there are often more than two options. The authorities can be summoned. With the ubiquity of cameras, it is not hard to provide evidence of what happened. One can also approach the perpetrator and share some words. Such a conversation cannot include threats, but it may certainly convey a message of "Shame on you!" Of course, any such conversation does increase the likelihood of violence developing. In such a case, we must ask ourselves the purpose of the conversation. This brings us to our final condition for entry into justified violence.

---

20. The reader would be wise to do a little research before assuming which candidate each side supported.

Good Intention

Just war theory requires not only proper authority and a just cause for a war to be justified, it also requires "good intention." The same applies to interpersonal violence among civilians. While the law may be satisfied if we can show just cause, morality sets higher standards. Intent and motivation play a very important role.

Saint Thomas Aquinas believed that a person can use violence in the act of self-defense. However, if one person strikes another "in anger," he regarded such an act as "brawling," which Thomas believed to be a mortal sin. "[B]rawls are included in St. Paul's works of the flesh and *those who behave like this will not inherit the kingdom of God.*"[21] The motivation and intention behind the action are important.

Thomas continues, "In the man who defends himself it may be without any sin, it may involve venial sin, or it may even be a mortal sin, all depending on what is going on in his mind and his manner of self-defence. If his sole idea is to withstand the injury intended for him and he defends himself with restraint, then there is no sin. Properly speaking, he is not engaged in a brawl. If, however, he is moved by vengeance or hatred and goes beyond the appropriate restraint, then it is always a sin."[22]

Thus, in determining whether or not to fight, we must be honest with ourselves. In the story related above, where the man followed me to the gas station, I could easily have justified violence as self-defense. The guy had followed me, blocked my exit, threatened me, and was poking me in the chest. However, insofar as I did not perceive a need to use violence to defend myself, I would have been morally wrong to engage in it. I honestly did not believe myself to be in any danger. Popping him in the nose may have felt vindicating; it would have made a good story for my friends. However, my intention in that case would be self-serving. I would be choosing violence in order to feel good about myself—either as a "champion of justice" or something of a badass. I would not have acted with the intent to "secure peace" or "promote the good." I would have been acting contrary to ideals of *shalom/salaam.*

When the legal threshold justifying violence has been reached, we must still ask ourselves about our intent. Is the reason for violence in this situation to keep myself and/or others safe? Or is this about wanting to brawl, to teach someone a lesson, or to feel good about myself? To be sure, honest introspection is not easy—especially in a high-adrenaline situation

---

21. Aquinas, *Summa Theologica* 2a2æ 41, 1.
22. Aquinas, *Summa Theologica* 2a2æ 41, 1.

when we may have only seconds to think and act. Also, as discussed previously, our motivations are multiple. We do things for a variety of reasons. A violent act may be morally justified and personally gratifying at the same time. However, if we ever choose to act in self-defense, and find ourselves delighting in handing out our own brand of justice, it is important to keep ourselves in check the whole time. Only the motivation to protect one's safety should determine what physical acts follow. Luther advised never to fight unless you can say, "My neighbor compels and forces me to fight, though I would rather avoid it."[23]

Nevertheless, there are times when we take actions that we know may provoke violence. For example, if I see someone behaving very rudely to another person in a public setting, and the victim cannot stick up for himself, I might walk up to the discourteous individual and explain that the behavior was rude and that he should apologize. No threat of violence is implied, but we all know that my action does increase the chances of violence happening. So, again, what is my intent? To stop bullying behavior or provoke a fight?

There are times when nonviolently confronting someone who is engaged in misdeeds is perfectly legal and can serve the purpose of stopping the bad behavior. An agitator who is harassing others may need some deterrent to his bad behavior. To repeat,

> Most bad guys resort to violence expecting to have no bad consequences, and they are usually right. Unless someone steps in (and is willing to risk all that comes on the line in a violent encounter), most low-level violence is rewarded, not punished. Civilians can, and often do, look the other way.[24]

In the immortal words of Edmund Burke, "The only thing necessary for the triumph of evil is for good men to do nothing." Here, we are not talking about vigilantism, but the willingness to stand up and say something.

While I do not wish to overstate the situations in which we generally find ourselves, the reflection of Martin Niemöller (1892–1984), who waited too long to oppose the Nazis, is also relevant here:

> First they came for the Socialists, and I did not speak out—
> Because I was not a Socialist.
>   Then they came for the Trade Unionists, and I did not
> speak out—Because I was not a Trade Unionist.
>   Then they came for the Jews, and I did not speak out—
> Because I was not a Jew.

23. Luther, "Whether Soldiers, Too, Can be Saved," 121.
24. Miller and Kane, *Scaling Force*, 63.

Then they came for me—and there was no one left to speak
for me.

I am wary here of engaging in a *Reductio ad Hitlerum* argument. My
point is not that the troublemakers we face in our lives should be compared
to Nazis. Rather, it is important to recognize that bad behavior which goes
unchecked may lead to worse behavior. In itself, it is creating some reward
for the offender. It may be helpful to introduce some cost as well. That cost
may be public shaming or a warning. The willingness to stand up for others, and vocally to condemn misconduct, can be a deterrent—both to the
perpetrator as well as future perpetrators among the witnesses. It can also
encourage and provide comfort to the victim of the initial aggression.

Imagine some teenagers hanging out in a park. A young black girl
passes by and is called "nigger" by the group, to the sound of laughter. A
postal worker or little old lady who overhears this may walk up to the offenders and strongly condemn the bullies: "That's wrong! Stop it!" Doing
so does risk the possibility of violence, and it may not shame the boys into
never doing it again, but it might very well have a positive effect. It also
signals something very important to the target of the abuse about the community she lives in: not everyone feels this way or will turn a blind eye to
it. Many of us would see a response along these lines as a moral imperative.

At the same time, the road to hell is paved with good intentions. Very
often we convince ourselves we are doing some greater good when we are
actually making things worse. The example of Leo Gaje comes to mind
again. And even when we do not escalate to unwarranted violence, our
desire to "teach someone a lesson" with our words and bravado can have
negative consequences. It is not far to go from "Watch your mouth" to "I'm
gonna knock that loud mouth out!" Keeping one's own temper in check is
enough of a challenge, to say nothing of your control over another's temper.

Unworthy Intentions

As discussed above, confronting another person carries certain risks to one's
own welfare. There are times, however, when a person actually desires an
escalation to violence. The "bad" guy may be provoking me, but I also may
be provoking him. If I approach someone who acted rudely to my wife, to
tell him that such behavior is not socially acceptable, I may actually want
him to throw a punch. It would give me the opportunity to settle things the
way I want. My intention here may not be to deter future bad behavior on
his part as much as to defend the honor of both my wife and myself. I'm just
smart enough not to walk up and jack him in the jaw.

There is a video on the internet showing a man on a motorcycle who was passed on the road by a very aggressive driver. The motorcyclist followed him to a Walmart parking lot, parked next to him, and started a "conversation" with him about his driving. He videotaped the entire exchange. The driver of the car turned out to be, perhaps, the worst person in the world. He made quite a few colorful remarks about the motorcyclist's mother and kept escalating the nastiness. If you have ever wanted to see someone get punched in the face, it was this guy. The videographer did a remarkable job of not losing his cool, but he kept talking to the driver, keeping him going and egging him on. He clearly knew the law, and never threatened the driver. He stayed within the letter of the law, but after a while it became clear that he was waiting for the other guy to step over the line and become a threat. When the reckless driver finally did, punches were thrown.

In such a case, it is pretty clear that the "good guy" wanted to brawl. Even if it was physically initiated by the other guy, his intentions are pretty clear to the viewer. The Greek philosopher Isidore (c. 450–c. 520) discussed three attributes of those who are brawlers:

1. They are "always ready to contradict" what others say or do.

2. They "delight in fighting."

3. They "stir up contention," provoking others into situations where violence is likely to result.

Thomas Aquinas wrote about these characteristics of the brawler, quoting God's warning in Proverbs 28:25 about "He that boasts and puffs himself up [and] stirs up quarrels."[25] And Martin Luther clarified, as quoted at the beginning of Part Four, the time when it is right to resort to violence: "Wait until the situation compels you to fight when you have no desire to do so."[26]

In the end, unfortunately, we are not left with a clear line to draw. We recognize that calling out bad behavior can provoke violence. We commend those with the courage to act, realizing that they put themselves in danger. However, courage can prompt us to both virtuous and vicious behavior. Certainly the desire for a situation to devolve into violence is not praiseworthy. On the other hand, the one who is prepared for that contingency, while hoping to avoid it, may be applauded for both her intentions and actions. Even then, behaviors with good intentions can still make a bad situation worse.

25. Aquinas, *Summa Theologica* 2a2æ 41, 1, ad. 1.
26. Luther, "Whether Soldiers, Too, Can be Saved," 118.

Creating "Bad Intentions" For Doing Good

Generally speaking, we want to create good intentions in ourselves and in others. I argued earlier that we should seek to be peacemakers, to create *shalom, salaam*. A person with good intentions does not seek out violence, but works for peace. Bad intentions would appear to be unequivocally—well, bad. However, can "bad intentions" ever be good? In a case where a virtuous person has determined that violence is necessary and right, the violent act needs to be carried out effectively. Timidity or half-measures are not more honorable, but quite the opposite. Timorousness can lead to greater harm, not less. In the words of Teddy Roosevelt, "Don't hit at all if it is honorably possible to avoid hitting; but never hit soft!"

Thus, to speak of creating "bad intentions," I am not using the word "bad" in an ethical sense. Here, "bad intentions" are not morally corrupt, but the intention is to engage in an activity that significantly harms another human being. This is different than the desire to revel in another's suffering.

Lieutenant Colonel David Grossman's book *On Killing* drew a great deal of attention to the odd phenomenon that soldiers often fail to try and kill the enemy during war.[27] They often shoot over the heads of their enemies; they freeze; they drop their guns to help out with other activities. In fact, the more that violence is face-to-face, the more difficult it is to engage. As discussed in chapter 4, shooting a person with a rifle is psychologically harder than firing at a vehicle. In turn, driving a knife into a man's body is a lot harder than firing a rifle at him.

Of course, we know that soldiers need to be able to do their jobs. The work may be unpleasant, disturbing or even "polluting," but if the cause is just, the violence needs to happen. However, even in the "Good War," Grossman claims that only 15–20 percent of American riflemen fired at the enemy during World War II.[28] Even if this number is underestimated by half, it was still an unacceptable percentage when conducting a war. Allied soldiers needed to hit their enemies, and they needed to hit them hard.

If this is the case with soldiers who have been trained to fight, how much more difficult would it be for an average citizen to try to maim or kill another human being up close and personal? Yet, this is where civilian self-defense takes place! Unless one is a pacifist, it is conceivable that you or

27. There are, admittedly, some shortcomings in Grossman's work, and plenty of criticism of his arguments. Nevertheless, his observations are still meaningful, even if one contests some of his statistics and conclusions.

28. Grossman, *On Killing*, 4. Grossman cites US Army Brigadier General S. L. A. Marshall for this statistic.

I might face a situation when such a level of violence is called for. How does one flip that switch?

Please note: I am not talking about barroom brawls or testosterone-fueled pissing contests. Rather, imagine that someone breaks into your home at night, where your children are sleeping, carrying a crowbar and two rolls of duct tape. Or consider the possibility of a man twice your size grabbing you in a parking lot at night and pushing you into the back of his van. In such a case, most people generally believe you are justified in using whatever level of force is necessary to stop the threat. That may be deadly force, and deadly force is not pretty. In fact, it would turn the stomach of any normal person.

I often see self-defense lessons for women where the participants are taught to use their keys or pen to attack the eyes of an assailant. There are a number of serious reservations I have about these tactics. The first question that comes to mind is, "Could you really ram your metal key into and through the eyeball of another human being?" Most of us cannot. Moreover, a half-effort in that direction is likely to increase the danger and violence significantly that would be directed at the victim.

Grossman relates the story of a karate teacher who had his students simulate eye attacks by having the "attacker" hold two oranges over his eyes. As the "victim" stuck her fingers through the flesh of the fruit, the attacker would scream and jerk around.[29] There are some people who can do this with no reservations, but most of us would have a difficult time with it. Even if we think we can, our minds have been conditioned our entire lives to never do such a thing. That is hard to overcome.

This book is not the place to consider the different tactics that militaries have used to enable soldiers to fight and kill. The methods are various and controversial. However, it is worth considering what psychological techniques civilians might need to utilize to enable themselves to carry out dreadful acts of violence, when deemed necessary. It may be necessary to create "bad intentions."

Personally, I am the kind of person who does not like violence. I certainly hope I never find myself in a situation where I would need to use violence to defend myself or a family member. While I train in martial arts, I really do not like hurting people. Realizing that about myself, however, sometimes gives me pause. If the situation called for it, could I immediately "pull the trigger" to do what I believe to be right and necessary?

I realized a few years ago, however, that whenever I believe my children are in danger, something primitive and instinctive takes over. One night

29. Grossman, *On Killing*, 132.

at home, I suddenly perceived a danger at our front door while my sons and I were watching TV together. Without any deliberation or hesitation, I headed fearlessly in that direction ready to fight.[30] On the other hand, if I am by myself, that same instinctive reaction is not present. After observing this, I realized that I could create this trigger—even when alone—by imagining any perceived danger to myself as a danger to my children. If I need that strong "fight" mechanism, I can elicit it in this way.

At the same time, I worried that such a strong emotional stimulus might leave me overly-aggressive, so that I might exceed the level of violence that would be necessary in a situation. I had the chance to ask Sergeant Rory Miller about this at a seminar in Tokyo in 2015. His response was that if I decide to think about my children in order to enable myself to act in a situation of self-defense, I would still maintain the mental clarity to avoid overkill. Moreover, I would also be inclined to avoid behavior that I could not justify in front of them. If the trigger is the protection of my children, it is unlikely to lead to pure uncontrolled rage and violence. Imagining them there, in that context, could therefore also generate a curb on extreme violence.

For the person who desires to act ethically, but recognizes that this may someday require disturbing acts of violence, honest consideration of one's potential to engage in that violence is essential. It is necessary that we recognize what we are capable of doing, and what we are not. If psychological hacks are deemed helpful to overcome the natural resistance to extreme violence, we must be sure that we are the ones who control those mechanisms, and not the other way around.[31]

For civilians, the decision to engage in violence often happens with very little time for moral reflection or consultation. It often happens in unfamiliar contexts with unfamiliar people. Such a situation, moreover, is generally accompanied by a great deal of adrenaline, which interferes with hearing, peripheral vision, blood pressure, breathing, and clear thinking. The more one has considered the moral dimensions of potential situations

---

30. In that case, it turned out to be Christmas carolers who had snuck up on our front porch, not realizing that I could hear them whispering right outside our front door, before they rang the doorbell.

31. Marc MacYoung teaches people a particular mental hack, designed to put one in the mindset necessary to keep oneself alive. One should not think, "I need to defend myself against him." Rather, the mental directive must be "Him-Down-Now!" Kris Wilder has suggested a more dehumanizing adaptation, "It-Down-Now!" Dana Sheets pointed out to me that such an approach may work well in self-defense contexts for men, but less so for women who may find an assault beginning with both people on the ground. I do not wish to suggest one perfect mental hack, but point out the complexity of the relationship between individual psychology and self-defense.

beforehand, the more one can make reasonable and defensible decisions in the moment. We do not want to "hit the switch" on "bad intentions" when the situation does not merit it. Reading a book is helpful, but not enough. To achieve excellence in anything—morality no less than others—practice is necessary. This is the theme to which we will return in detail in the final section of this book.

CHAPTER 8

How to Fight

Jus in Bello

Quarrel like people who know that one day they will be reconciled.

—PLATO

Considerations of *how* one ought to engage in violence, within the context of civilian self-defense, are distinct but not totally dissimilar from the rules that govern warfare. Therefore, we will look at the three dominant criteria for *jus in bello* to consider their relevance and relation to the violence that individual civilians may face. In discussing *discrimination*, *proportionality*, and *due care*, it is the latter two that have the most applicability to this context, and will therefore be the foci of the majority of this chapter.

Discrimination

The principle of discrimination, as discussed in chapter 5, deals primarily with the moral responsibility to discriminate between combatants and non-combatants. The US Army's publication "The Soldier's Rules" states the following: "Soldiers fight only enemy combatants. Soldiers do not harm enemies who surrender. Soldiers do not kill or torture enemy prisoners of war."[1] The intentional targeting of civilians is prohibited.

---

1. As in Johnson, *Ethics and the Use of Force*, 89.

This obviously has little connection with situations where civilians may need to defend themselves. As explosive as your fighting style may be, you are unlikely to create collateral damage. Likewise, it is difficult to imagine that a rational person would punch an innocent bystander to demoralize an opponent. In fights between individuals, it is usually pretty clear who is a combatant, and who is not. Those who "surrender," in war or self-defense, are to be treated as non-combatants. Hostilities must end when the aggressor is no longer posing a threat, as we discussed previously. For the most part, the principle of discrimination has little connection to the violence which civilians face.

The one exception to this may be cases where a firearm is brought to bear. While punches and kicks are unlikely to overreach their targets and injure others (although there are exceptions; e.g., Exod 21:22), the same is not true of bullets. A situation that may justify shooting another human being in self-defense is likely to require consideration of where the bullets go. To what extent are innocent passersby put in jeopardy by the exercise of your right to self-defense? This, however, is more closely related to the consideration of *due care*, which we will consider below.

Proportionality

The principle of proportionality is important when considering the ethics of civilian self-defense. If a situation requires the use of violence to keep oneself or others safe, it does not follow that any and all acts of physical force are justified. Any response must be measured by the relative danger of the situation. If someone "gets in your face," you are not justified in breaking a few bones and joints, stomping the groin, gouging the eyes, re-stomping the groin, etc.[2] The response must be proportionate to the threat. If someone is about to give you an "educational beatdown,"[3] you should not raise the stakes to a potentially fatal encounter.

When I was a student at Vanderbilt Divinity School, I was the goal-keeper for our coed intramural soccer team. One evening we were playing a spirited game with the Law School when things went a little haywire. After a significant collision with one of the opposing female players, she

2. As we discussed in the previous chapter, someone who "gets in your face" may not be sufficient cause to use violence at all, unless one perceives an imminent attack on the part of the aggressor.

3. An "educational beatdown" is what Miller and Kane define as "sort of a spanking between adults, an extreme show of displeasure designed to enforce the 'rules'" (*Scaling Force*, 16).

was knocked down and I was left standing. (For the record, she was the one at fault.) The men on her team took exception to my behavior (even though she was the one who ran into me. Honestly!). I was approached by a couple of them, words were exchanged, and one of them grabbed me by my sleeve. Fortunately, things simmered down from there and nothing more happened. However, if one had taken a swing at me, a proportional response might have been to take a swing back. That may not have been the wisest choice, but it would be proportional. If, on the other hand, I had pulled out a knife and stabbed him, I would have clearly exceeded the principle of proportionality—even though he had started the fight.

The law makes it clear that you may defend yourself to the point of stopping a threat, but then no further. (This also relates to "discrimination," if the former assailant is now considered to have "surrendered.") An assailant "forfeits" his right to be safe from physical harm when he is in the process of attacking you; at that time, you may respond to the attack with violence of your own.[4] However, that forfeiture only lasts for the duration of the assault. Once an assailant has stopped his assault, you may not continue to use violence against him. If you continue to do so, you are now the one committing assault, for which you are at fault both legally and morally. When an assailant has stopped attacking, the victim must cease all violence directed at him, despite how unfair that may feel.

Imagine if the scuffle at the soccer game had really gone sour. The angry teammate might have thrown a punch, and I might have punched him back, knocking him to the ground where he remained holding his face in his hands. I could not then proceed to kick him in the ribs. When the threat stops, so must you. If, on the other hand, he looked up at me in a fit of anger and spit out in rage "Now I'm really going to kill you!" then a hard kick in the side of the thigh might be a good idea, followed by my sprinting across the field.

It is important to recognize that even if one's response is proportional, this may still lead to an escalation of violence. If a drunk in a bar throws a punch at me for looking at his girlfriend, a proportional response might be to duck and hit him back. However, his friends might then get involved, and now I would be facing a very serious and threatening reality. Likewise, a woman who hits a groper in the face is unable to then escape the situation, she may now be in danger of greater physical harm. In these cases, the level of response may be proportional, but the dynamics of the situation

---

4. For a detailed examination of the word "forfeiture," and some of the questions it raises, see Lang, "Why Not Forfeiture?"

can mean that an equivalent response creates a significantly more violent altercation. This is not in accord with the principle of proportionality.

No one can perfectly predict what will happen when a choice is made in a violent scenario, but one must at least be mindful of the interpersonal dynamics involved so that a reasonable course of action may be pursued. Any act of self-defense should be carried out with a reasonable expectation of ending the violence, not escalating it.

The reader will recall that, when we discussed proportionality in just war theory, there were Christians who granted that force may be met by force; however, charity demands that the use of less force is preferable. Grotius argued that believers should be restrained by "good wishes" for one's enemies, not taking advantage of their own full right to respond with equal force.[5] A particular use of force may be advantageous, but it may not be necessary.[6] Love of neighbor may demand that one respond with less force than one faces—perhaps as little as possible.

However, there is a problem here. Just as we saw with cases of war, the attempt to use a less violent response can sometimes lead to greater harm than good. In the words of Prussian General Helmut von Moltke, "The greatest kindness in war is to bring it to a speedy conclusion."[7] A less-than-overwhelming response may only make the conflict last longer. A delay in resolution may leave time for the violence to escalate or others to join the fray. Sometimes the most merciful thing to do is to end things quickly. Those who remember the Gulf War may recall the Powell Doctrine, which seeks to make the most effective use of one's resources to end the fighting quickly. This can appear to be a violation of proportionality, as was argued prior to General Powell's devastating attack on Iraq in 1991. Archbishop John Roach raised this criticism during the military buildup,[8] but Powell was clearly vindicated when his approach secured an end to hostilities, with far fewer casualties than anyone expected, after only five weeks of fighting.

Proportionality and Christian charity must be understood with appreciation for the fact that hitting quick and hitting hard can sometimes resolve a situation more quickly than half-measures. When I was in middle school, I went through a troublesome phase, shall we say. One day in seventh grade, trying to establish my masculine *bona fides*—to others as well as to myself—I picked a fight with Mark, who lived down the street. I didn't really like Mark, but he had done nothing wrong on this day. After we got off

---

5. Johnson, *Ethics and the Use of Force*, 81.

6. Lee, *Ethics and War*, 127.

7. Walzer, *Just and Unjust Wars*, 47.

8. Johnson, *Ethics and the Use of Force*, 99.

the bus, we put our backpacks down and squared off. I threw one punch at his stomach, and he hit me three times in the face. As I backed off, he asked me if I was finished. I don't recall making any reply, but he just picked up his bag and headed home.

Was his response proportional? I threw one punch at his stomach, but he hit me three times in the face. His actions were, of course, more aggressive and violent than mine (and remarkably fast, as I recall!). However, by bringing more force to bear immediately, he also ended the conflict more quickly. To end a violent encounter, one often needs to get ahead of the escalation of violence in order to stop it. Notice, however, that he did not jump the force continuum a few steps, but just enough to end the conflict.

I learned a number of valuable lessons that day. First, don't lead with a punch to the body; it leaves your face open. Second, don't pick a fight with a kid who has a bunch of older brothers, especially if you don't have any. Third, and most importantly, winning graciously can stop any future return to hostility. Mark didn't taunt me, and social media didn't exist at that time, so there was no record of our fisticuffs. He walked away and that was the end of things. While I was disappointed, to say the least, I never held any ill will toward him after that.

Sometimes a situation offers the possibility of a response which relies on a lower level of violence right off the bat. There are times when one can end an encounter in creative ways with a response that uses less force than is already in play. A video on the internet shows a group of people on a train in Europe, where a man starts verbally assaulting a female passenger. Another man, sitting opposite the woman, quickly gets up and yanks down the sweatpants of the aggressor. The pantsed-man turns around and realizes that he is outmatched in size by the clever pantser, who looks ready to go if things escalate. He sheepishly pulls up his pants and walks off. Given the particular context, this was probably the quickest return to *shalom/salaam* on that train possible.

The larger man resolved the situation with a minimal use of force. His quick thinking and imposing physique permitted a minimal use of force, easily satisfying the requirement of proportionality. If, on the other hand, the initial aggressor had been larger than the second man, this tactic would likely have been an invitation to immediate physical violence. Creating such a scenario would not have been a proportional tactic. A proper response stops the violence within proportional means; it does not stimulate an escalation of violence.

Another story, which I related in my book *When Buddhists Attack*, illustrates the challenge of proportionality. It involved a former military man who was attacked by a teenager with a knife. As a result of his training, he was able to defend himself effectively, disarm the young man, seize the knife, and barely stopped himself before stabbing the boy in the eye.[9] In this case, while a young man with a knife can be a very dangerous adversary, the skill and size of the adult, coupled with his disarming of the boy, meant that stabbing him with his own knife would have been a profound violation of proportionality.

In contemplating proportionality with regard to personal self-defense, one must consider what is at stake in the situation. Unlike in warfare, not every violent physical encounter involves a mortal threat. The ability to differentiate various situations and determine the level of threat involved is of tremendous value when deciding how to act. The wrong response to a situation can lead to a needless escalation of violence, or (conversely) to an inadequate response to a deadly threat.

Social Violence

An "educational beatdown" is a situation where one party feels the need to "teach a lesson" to another. This is a type of social violence. Here, there are unspoken rules that govern the violence and the desired social outcome. The goal here may not be benevolent, but it is intended as educational. While it may be quite violent, it is not intended to be life-threatening. Consider a situation where a clumsy individual knocks over the motorcycle of a Hell's Angel in a parking lot. The ungainly fellow would certainly offer profuse apologies to the menacing and angry biker. However, he may still get the opportunity to learn a lesson about respect for others' property. If he is unable to flee, he is better off just to "take his lumps." The gang member is not intending to kill him in this situation. Any effort to escalate things to protect himself—for example, by pulling a weapon—would likely end far worse for him and others involved. Such a reaction would not be proportional to the situation.

A more common form of social violence is the "monkey dance." This is the "ritualized combat between males to safely establish dominance without the likelihood of crippling injury or death."[10] The classic example involves two young men in a bar and witty banter like "What are you looking at?" or "You want a piece of me?" Such situations can play out in many other places, of course, like fraternity houses, street corners, or gas stations after a traffic misunderstanding. They are often accompanied by physical displays: chests are inflated, arms are spread wide, and faces come closer to each other than

9. Mann, *When Buddhists Attack*, 73.
10. Miller and Kane, *Scaling Force*, 15.

men normally feel comfortable with. (Interestingly, these are all the exact opposite of an effective fighting strategy.)

If fighting results, it will often go on to the point where one person is knocked out, one participant submits, or others break up the fight. As in the educational beatdown, the goal is social dominance, not the death or maiming of the other. Again, certain unspoken rules are in play. Groin shots, biting, and eye-gouging are frowned upon. Assistance from another is viewed negatively. The introduction of a weapon is highly inappropriate. This is not to say that these things never happen, but that the monkey dance usually plays out with a lower level of violence.

Just as an educational beatdown often requires its victim to endure the mistreatment or run away, the monkey dance is usually best ended without a recourse to violence. It requires intelligence, social skills, and humility. If you accidentally knock into someone in a bar who then starts the dance, rather than become his dancing partner, it is wiser to offer an apology: "Hey, I'm sorry. It's been a long day and I was thinking about something else. Let me buy you a beer."

Sometimes, however, the violence begins before you have a chance to diffuse it. A looping right hook may arrive immediately after a conversation starter. Despite our best efforts to avoid trouble, trouble can find any of us. In such a situation, one may feel the need and justification to fight back. Proportionality demands that one play by the rules of the game. In a case of social violence, the rules of social violence must be observed. Pulling out brass knuckles in a low-stakes monkey dance is not a proportionate response. As discussed previously with regard to just war theory, "The level of our response is thus limited by considerations of proportionality: we ought to do no more to the other than he was prepared to do to us."[11]

Even when a significant escalation of violence is perceived to increase your chances of "winning," it can be both immoral and imprudent to do so. From an ethical standard, escalating the violence in order not to "lose" a fight means that there will likely be greater suffering. You may comfort yourself believing that the additional suffering may all belong to the "bad" guy. However, the intentional maiming, disfigurement, or killing of another human being as punishment for picking a fight is not defensible. It creates far more harm than good for all involved. It requires one person to exempt himself from the social rules, making an exception for himself that he would not extend to the other. Escalation of violence also corrupts one's character, as acts of unnecessary violence always will. Such acts move us away from the desired goal of being peacemakers; they further undermine the *shalom/*

---

11. Johnson, *Ethics and the Use of Force*, 81.

salaam we have a moral obligation to build in society. From the perspectives of utilitarian, deontological, and virtue ethics, escalating violence out of proportion to a situation is immoral.

Even if we consider this from a purely self-interested standpoint, it is unwise. The individual who knocks over the Hell's Angel's motorcycle may get slapped around. If, however, he pulls a knife, all hell is going to break loose. In such a case we can consider the possible consequences of doing so:

1. He "wins" the encounter with the first biker, and is then killed by the rest.

2. He "wins" the encounter and escapes; the next day his house is mysteriously burned down and his dog is killed.

3. He "wins" and avoids retribution at the hands of the gang, but faces criminal and civil charges that use up his family's financial resources— even if he wins the case.

4. He loses the fight and is sent to the hospital with life-threatening injuries.

In any case, his escalation was extremely foolish.

Some years ago, I attended a martial arts seminar where one of the instructors presented a (literally) crippling combination of counter-attacks based on an initial punch by the "bad" guy. A number of these counters were designed to humiliate the other guy and break quite a few bones and joints along the way. I raised the question of "overkill," but my concerns were impolitely dismissed. The response was something to the effect of, "Maybe a more limited response may work in your sheltered world, but in *my* super badass neighborhood, we have to be prepared to take people down!" It is true that my neighborhood is safer than his. However, this is actually a reason for him to be more measured in his response. If someone throws a punch in a situation of social violence, and the response is to cripple the person, folks in his neighborhood are not going to let that slide. Much more than in my neighborhood, he may likely have someone gunning for him the next day. A proportional response means playing by the rules, and doing so maintains a certain level of mutual respect. One person's escalation today may lead to an additional escalation tomorrow.

Asocial Violence

Unlike the cases of social violence discussed above, there are different situations where your life may be in serious jeopardy. Someone may want to rape and kill you, take you to a secluded place and torture you, or drive a blade into your kidney just for the thrill of it. Sometimes people just temporarily lose their minds and viciously attack others in a rage. When faced with mortal danger, the ethical rules do not change, but the situation has. Proportionality still applies, but now a lethal response to a lethal threat is proportional.

An attack that is intended to maim or kill justifies a proportional response. If a person in a dark alley pulls a knife with the intent of using it on you, pulling a gun and shooting him until he stops is justified. If someone attempts to force you into a vehicle, even without a weapon, you are in the midst of one of the most dangerous situations you can face. People rarely return from such a ride. Any and every measure to keep yourself safe is legally and morally justified.

Escalation of violence is also permissible in this situation, and may be the wisest choice. If a larger person is trying to severely beat you into unconsciousness with his hands, you are acting reasonably and ethically when you grab a tire iron or broken bottle to fight back. Proportionality must take account of intentions, not just the tools. When the United States went to war with the Taliban, no one was suggesting that the military limit its use of weapons to those comparable to what the Taliban possessed. In a potentially lethal encounter, we should use the best tools at our disposal to end things as quickly as possible.

I recently heard of a man who was attacked while in prison. His attacker was punching and kicking him severely. He honestly—and probably correctly—perceived his life to be in danger. When he got the chance, he bit an entire chunk of flesh out of his attacker's calf muscle. As a result, he survived. In cases of asocial violence, when one perceives life or limb to be in jeopardy, any response directed at the attacker is proportional. Furthermore, engaging in high levels of violence to end the threat immediately sometimes achieves a greater end for all involved.

The following example is not actually asocial violence, but carries with it the same danger. It is sometimes known as the "group monkey dance." Here, what starts out as a form of social violence can easily accelerate and spiral out of control. A social or educational beatdown is joined by others and quickly escalates uncontrollably, even though no one present made a conscious decision to engage in extreme violence. Friends or bystanders may throw their lot in with one side, encouraging one another into increasing acts of brutality, and an ecstatic escalation of viciousness results. Readers may consider the fate of Simon in *Lord of the Flies* or the countless victims of mob violence around the world that make the news every day. The offenders rarely plan to carry out atrocities; they just happen. Miller and Kane explain,

"Unlike an individual monkey dance, the group monkey dance can easily end with a murder, even when killing the victim was not the goal."[12]

Also, unlike what happens in the movies, a single individual—regardless of how well-trained—is highly unlikely to win a fight against three or more opponents. If a group is attacking one person, the only logical recourse is flight. Simply running away, however, is not always that easy. One may need to engage in an act of serious violence to facilitate one's escape. Ramming a key into a person's eye, stomping a knee perpendicular to its normal range of motion, or smashing the butt end of a stick through a person's clavicle, are all highly violent acts. In this context, however, such a violent act—along with the consequent screaming it creates—may buy one enough time to escape. The only other option, realistically, may simply be to remain and possibly be killed. One may not have the stomach to engage in such acts, and we should be honest with ourselves about what we are capable of. However, if people are about to kill you, proportionality permits anything you deem necessary to stop the attack that the assailants are attempting.

Due Care

Ankō Itosu (1831–1915) was a famous karate teacher from Okinawa, and remains a legend among martial artists to this day. In one account, told by his student Gichin Funakoshi, Itosu was attacked on the street:

> Indeed, Itosu was so well trained that his entire body seemed to be invulnerable. Once, as he was about to enter a restaurant in Naha's amusement center, a sturdy young man attacked him from the rear, aiming a hearty blow at his side. But the latter, without even turning, hardened the muscles of his stomach so that the blow glanced off his body, and at the very same instant his right hand grasped the right wrist of his assailant. Still without turning his head, he calmly dragged the man inside the restaurant.
>
> There, he ordered the frightened waitress to bring food and wine. Still holding the man's wrist with his right hand, he took a sip of the wine from the cup that he held in his left hand, then pulled his assailant around in front of him and for the first time had a look at him. After a moment, he smiled and said, "I don't know what your grudge against me could be, but let's have a

12. Miller and Kane, *Scaling Force*, 16.

drink together!" The young man's astonishment at his behavior can easily be imagined.[13]

Itosu, in this interesting story, would have been legally and morally permitted to have struck his assailant. In the social and political context of late nineteenth-century Okinawa, he may have been justified in leaving the man crippled or dead. However, Itosu exercised what we might call "due care."

The practice of "due care" does not necessarily mean nonviolence. Itosu did not just absorb the strike and run away. He manhandled the young ruffian with significant, albeit well-controlled, force. What he did was use the least amount of violence necessary to achieve the desired result—a safe resolution to an assault with the prospect of greater peace in the future. Proportionality would have permitted a heavy-handed response, but it was due care that prompted Itosu to find a better solution. While Itosu never read Saint Thomas or Grotius, his conduct was in keeping with the principle they taught: "Even under such circumstances the one who is attacked ought to prefer to do anything possible to frighten away or weaken the assailant, rather than cause his death."[14]

There are times when the choice to engage in extreme violence may actually be the right thing to do, as we have seen above. However, this must be balanced by the third principle within *jus in bello*, "due care." While defending oneself and others may require brutal acts, which can be morally justified if truly necessary, these should always be moderated by due care for the assailant. As in cases of war, "Moral consideration should be given not just to the killing of combatants, but to their suffering as well."[15] Here is where charity demands that one must consider the well-being of the guilty party. An end to hostilities is not the only objective of the ethical person, but the effort to create a better and safer future for all involved.

To begin with, one should cause the least harm possible. While proportionality may sometimes justify striking someone in the face with your fist, it may be preferable to pin him to the ground with a joint lock without injuring him. While a situation may warrant lethal force, if the threat can be neutralized with non-lethal force, "due care" requires that such an effort be made. Lee explains, "Least harm . . . allows an action be taken only if there is no less harmful action that could be taken instead to achieve the same . . . objective."[16]

13. Funakoshi, *Karate-Do*, 16.

14. Grotius, *On the Law of War and Peace*, 83.

15. Lee, *Ethics and War*, 221.

16. Lee, *Ethics and War*, 218.

Many years ago I had a training partner at Vanderbilt University named Ken. He was a very fine martial artist, an easygoing guy, and something of a genius.[17] He once related to me a story wherein he had entered a convenience store one night, only to find a situation of escalating violence between a few customers. There was a large muscular guy with a big mouth stirring up the trouble, and somehow Ken got pulled into the conflict. When the larger fellow made a hostile move toward him, Ken responded with a single kick to the outside of the aggressor's thigh. As it happens, Ken was a student of Muay Thai, a martial art that is famous for its brutal leg-kicks. The bully in the store stepped back, with his eyes wide with a bit of confusion. He had never encountered such a kick before. He wasn't sure how it was thrown or how to defend against it. What he did know was that his leg hurt—a lot! It was stiffening up and difficult to walk on. He certainly did not want to receive a second dose of that medicine. As a result, he disengaged the situation and limped out the door.

In this situation, Ken could have responded with a proportionate response that far exceeded a single kick to the thigh. He could have responded with the same level of violence that was about to be directed at him, and knocked the guy into next week. However, he chose one quick kick that would cause no injury, but would communicate that this path was not a wise one for his opponent to wander down. He took due care to keep the violence to a minimum, but still kept himself and others present safe.

Due care also demands that we consider the long-term effects of the violence we engage in. There is a continuum of violence in the use of force. Wrestling people to the ground and holding them there, with little pain and no injury, is at one end of the spectrum. A single kick to the leg may move us further up the scale. Of course, not all striking is equal. A hard punch to the liver or solar plexus may stop someone from further aggression while not injuring the person. A right hook to the chin can knock someone unconscious and end the hostility, but leave the person with a concussion. A finger in the eye can scratch a cornea or worse. A full-power Muay Thai kick to the inside of the knee can blow out a person's ACL. At the same time, serious injuries are not limited to strikers. Grapplers have the ability to easily hyperextend elbows and knees or dislocate shoulders.

However, we should not be naïve. In the heat of the moment, a person defending herself may not have the luxury to consider various options to stopping her assailant. Even a well-trained fighter is not going to ponder all her options when considering the best response to an assault. Still, some consideration of the effects of her actions is a moral imperative. When Plato

---

17. He actually won the MacArthur "Genius Grant" in 2006.

wrote that we should fight like people who will one day be reconciled, he wanted us to consider the long-term effects of our actions. Do you really want someone to wake up each morning for the rest of his life and put in his glass eye, because you blinded him with your car key? Do you want a person to lose his job, and possibly his house, because you broke his arm and he can no longer work? Due care is not only about pain at the moment when force is used, but about the long-term consequences. Some may object that this sets up a moral standard that is too high and lofty. However, the path of moral virtue should never be understood as an easy one.

In 2015, Officer Jesse Kidder pulled over Michael Wilcox, a man who was believed to have just killed two people. Kidder was warned that the suspect was likely armed. When Wilcox failed to respond to orders to stop and put his hands up, but instead charged at the officer, a legal and moral threshold had been crossed. Officer Kidder would have been justified in shooting the man. Instead, he backed away, keeping his pistol trained on the suspect and repeating his orders. Wilcox continued making threatening gestures at Kidder, even telling him to shoot. Kidder's body camera captured the entire incident, as he made every effort not to use the force that was permitted him at that time. Eventually, Wilcox gave in and surrendered as other police arrived. Officer Kidder, like Itosu, chose the path that saved life, even when he would have been justified in taking it.

It is easy to commend those who follow the standard of due care, and promise ourselves that we will do likewise. However, there is a serious challenge and danger in doing so. It is important to acknowledge that what makes this principle a moral challenge is that it places people in danger. In fact, care for the enemy often places oneself (and others) at greater risk of harm.

Itosu took a risk when he dragged the young man with him to the restaurant. If the latter had a knife in his pocket, Itosu could have been stabbed and killed before they made it to their table. Officer Kidder exposed himself to the possibility that Wilcox could have charged him, taken his gun, and shot him. That would have left the community with a desperate and armed criminal, the police force with one fewer officer, and the Kidder family grieving the loss of a good young man.

The fact that adherence to the principle of due care may place one-self in more danger is not, however, a reason to reject it. A decision to act ethically often involves risk, harm, and loss. However, it is men and women of courage and moral fortitude, the ones who face severe dangers, who we recognize as those who improve the world which we share. The exercise of due care should not be undertaken carelessly, but it is a moral imperative that permits the best in humanity—where a person sacrifices her own interest for the sake of her enemy, and in the interest of a better future for us all.

An additional challenge is that even if we want to use the least violence necessary, it is tremendously difficult to identify where that point is. The problem with using minimal force to resolve a situation is that one rarely knows how much is necessary to stop a threat. I have trained with big, tough, muscular guys in an MMA gym who turned out to be horrible fighters with little resilience, and I have trained with women of modest stature in judo who looked rather unimpressive but could throw me around the dojo. When looking at a stranger, the fact that he is wearing a leather jacket or a pastel cardigan tells me nothing about how dangerous he is, and subsequently what level of force is necessary to stop him. If we add the possibility of mind-altering drugs to the equation, the situation becomes even more uncertain.

When I began martial arts, I was under the illusion that two solid punches to the face would simply knock a person down. Sometimes that works, but many times it does not. Fans of combat sports have seen fights where someone takes a significant number of skull-rattling shots to the head, barely flinches, and then smiles at her opponent as she stalks forward to return the favor. Other times, a glancing blow knocks an experienced fighter completely unconscious. This uncertainty also exists in street fights. People are sometimes lifted up and slammed to the ground, only to immediately bounce back up with no ill effects. Other times, they inadvertently hit their head on the street and die. In the midst of a high-adrenaline situation, when our mental clarity is obscured, it is extremely difficult to gauge what level of force is necessary to end the threat? Furthermore, a delay or hesitancy in a fight can mean the tables are turned and one's own life could be put in jeopardy.

In 2008, at the first Susquehanna Martial Arts Symposium, we hosted a lecture by our local district attorney on "self-defense and the law." One of the more interesting aspects of that presentation was an impassioned disagreement that arose between the district attorney and a rough-and-ready old karate teacher. The district attorney pointed out that people with martial arts experience—especially teachers—are held to a higher standard by the law. They should exercise greater levels of control when defending themselves. While this certainly makes sense, the old karate teacher correctly pointed out that one never knows how tough an assailant is. Trying to handle someone with kid gloves, when he could turn out to be a highly trained fighter himself—with a concealed weapon and friends nearby—is extremely dangerous. He argued that one needs to end the encounter as quickly as possible in order to keep oneself safe.

The conversation went back and forth for some time, with both men making valid arguments, and some frustration growing between them. In the end, the unfortunate reality is that there is no precise answer. On the one hand, the district attorney is right: people with greater fighting skills should be held to a higher standard. On the other, so was the karate teacher: you cannot take it easy on someone trying to hurt or maim you when you know nothing of their strengths, assets, and abilities. In the end, we must make the most measured assessment of a situation we can, knowing that we may be damned if we do, and damned if we don't. For the person who acts with good conscience (and has a good attorney) the chances are at least better that he will be exonerated by the law and society.

In observing the principle of "due care," it is important to remember that the object of civilian self-defense is to restore the *status quo ante*. That is, one is attempting to restore the safety of oneself and others that existed before any assault began. There is no room for punishment. There may often be the temptation to escalate to the point of proportionality, even when that level of response is not necessary. Due care requires generosity of spirit, and can mean placing oneself in greater danger. Due care is aided when we remember that punishment is a role for others. As discussed above, teaching someone a lesson is not defensible—legally or morally. By returning the same level of force in order to satisfy a desire for justice, revenge, or bravado, one has stepped over the line, failing to observe due care.

Firearms, Proportionality, and Due Care

Lastly, with regard to due care, we must say a word about firearms. The scope of this book is too limited to treat this subject with the depth it deserves. However, when discussing self-defense with firearms, considerations of proportionality and due care become much more critical. They also bear a closer resemblance to a military context. As soon as one straps on a pistol, or pulls a shotgun out from under the bed, a decision has been made that raises ethical, legal, and personal stakes tremendously. The same applies if one ever chooses to engage with an assailant who possesses a firearm.

For the individual with the gun, there is far less flexibility with regard to the amount of force that can be used. Things may quickly jump to a level of lethal force. If a scenario of social violence unfolds while I am in possession of a pistol, the stakes can immediately be raised to the highest level. What may have been limited to a scuffle can take a drastic turn if the other person observes—or gets ahold of!—my firearm. If I grab a shotgun in order to deal with a potentially dangerous situation on my property, I cannot simply drop it on the ground and deescalate to hand-to-hand fighting if I determine the threat level to be relatively low. The introduction of a firearm can have the effect of eliminating stages on the continuum of force. If force becomes necessary, it may well be deadly force.

In 2016, a mother in Portland, Oregon returned home one night with her two daughters (five and ten) to discover a man in the children's room. The mother pulled out her firearm and shot the intruder, fifty-nine-year-old David Daniel McCrary, killing him. In this case, McCrary—who had a history of mental illness—may have broken into the house looking for a place to sleep for the night, not hurt anyone. While it is not my intention to pass judgment on the mother's decision, the presence of the gun meant that the only force she could consider was fatally shooting the intruder.[18]

It is, of course, possible that the presence of a firearm can be a strong deterrent to violence. This happens all the time, and it almost never makes the news. If a petty thief breaks in the front door of a house and finds Grandma sitting on the steps with a double-barrel twelve-gauge shotgun pointed at him, a further crime is likely to be avoided. This particular incident happened in Boynton Beach, Florida, also in 2016, although the grandmother was holding a .22 caliber pistol. When three men broke into her house in the middle of the day, they found themselves looking down the barrel of the gun, while the grandmother yelled that she was going to shoot the "bastards." Their visit to her house lasted only about thirty seconds, as they quickly retreated back out the front door.

Flashing one's sidearm may deter a brawler from escalating his monkey dance to fisticuffs.[19] At the same time, trying to trump another's threat of aggression with one's own threat of maximum force remains a risky gambit when the initial threat was not at that level.

In most cases of civilian self-defense, collateral damage is not a concern. However, this is not the case with firearms. Bullets miss their target with great regularity; bullets hit their targets and pass through them; bullets ricochet and head off in all sorts of unintended directions. In all these cases, innocent bystanders—including one's own family members!—can be severely wounded or killed. One of the cardinal rules of gun safety is that you should always be sure of your target and what is behind it. However, self-defense situations often happen in the blink of an eye. There may be no time to survey one's environment. If someone pulls a knife on me in a

18. Those who suggest options like shooting him in the leg would greatly benefit from learning about the realities of self-defense with firearms.

19. Experts on gun safety differ as to whether it is ever acceptable to flash one's gun. It can indeed scare some people away, but it also allows the "bad guy" to know exactly what he or she is up against.

parking lot, I am likely to get tunnel vision and see nothing but that shiny flash of steel. Is there a minivan with a family pulling into a parking spot twenty feet behind him? Are there thirty cars stuck in traffic one hundred yards beyond that?

Due care when carrying a firearm requires much greater consideration of the safety of oneself, the assailant, and those in the area where the gun may be used. Very often, the best course of action will be retreat. Law enforcement officers, of course, do not have the luxury of retreat. While we civilians can find ourselves in comparably dangerous situations, it is important to remember that enforcement of the law is not our obligation. We must remember that personal safety is not about winning, but about not losing.

For those members of society who do purchase a handgun, it is imperative that they study its proper use for self-defense, practice until they have attained adeptness with the gun, and obtain the proper certification for concealed-carry. Everyone who decides to carry a firearm assumes a serious moral responsibility when they leave home armed. Carrying a firearm to defend oneself, one's family, and members of one's community is not about being a potential hero. It should be a daunting task. The possibility of killing another human being, or being targeted by others because of that gun, should give any reasonable person pause. Used properly, it can make one's society safer, but there is a heavy burden of responsibility as well. The person who does not feel that burden may want to reconsider carrying a firearm at all.

A Final Word

A final word on due care. When a nation removes landmines from its military arsenal, when non-lethal force is applied in a lethal situation, or when a fist is unclenched before the final blow, there is risk. There is also the potential for a far better future for all involved. However, due care should not be mistaken for either a lack of will or inability. In fact, those who have greater power are the ones with more options; those who lack skill and facility with violence have fewer choices.

Nations could give up carpet-bombing once they had more accurate weapons. Training and resources permit police to use non-lethal force. Ankō Itosu could only escort his assailant to the restaurant without injuring him because of many years of brutal training in the martial arts; a lesser man could not have handled the situation as courteously.

It is with this in mind, then, that we turn to considerations of self-cultivation. This often neglected topic is the true locus of how we can foster peace and improve our communities, creating *shalom/salaam*. This difficult undertaking is not simply a function of a good will, but also requires tremendous work to develop body, mind, and spirit. It is only then that we reach our moral and actual potential to live virtuous lives for the benefit of our neighbors.

PART FIVE

Self-Cultivation

The Dream is damned and Dreamer too if Dreaming's all that Dreamers do.

—RORY MILLER

Xenophon (435–354 BCE), the Greek philosopher and military commander, wrote this: "I notice that as those who do not train the body cannot perform the functions proper to the body, so those who do not train the soul cannot perform the functions of the soul." Cultivation of the whole self is necessary to achieve excellence of the whole self. If anyone wishes to make this world a better place, more is required than simply the desire to do so. An act of the will, not empowered by ability, is ineffective.

Whether your ethical convictions are nonviolent, pacifist, dovish, or hawkish, what we have in common is the desire to establish and increase peace—*shalom/salaam*. There is, however, a problem. It is not enough simply to assent to good ethical principles. The difficulty is that the labor to create peace is extremely demanding work. You may want to be a peacemaker, but do you have the tools to be one? Cultivation of these tools demands hard work that we are frequently unwilling to invest in.

Consider the following three questions:

What actions should my government take to help establish peace in Syria? An answer to this question requires a tremendous amount of knowledge about the history of that country; the cultures of its people; the political and religious contexts of its neighbors; and the international tensions among the various world powers who are being drawn into the conflict. To engage the peace process in Syria, we need to have spent considerable time learning about this country and its crisis.

If I see an apparently unstable man verbally assaulting a frightened individual on a bus, and threatening violence, what can I do to avoid needless bloodshed? Perhaps I can interpose my body between theirs and defuse the situation through a quiet strength. Possibly I can respond to violence with less violence, subduing rather than striking, controlling and pinning the man down until authorities arrive. Did I notice the knife he has concealed? Can I physically prevent him from drawing it and doing greater harm to those around us? To succeed in any of these possibilities, I need to have spent considerable time in physical training.

If some guy treats my wife with disrespect, right in front of me and my friends, and appears to be itching for a fight, how can I resolve this situation most appropriately? It would be wise to keep my pride in check. My desire to work toward a just peace is probably compromised by my desire to be the hand of justice. The best response in this situation will demand a significant amount of self-control and maturity on my part. If I am to act in accord with my ethical principles, I need to have spent considerable time cultivating my spirit.

The ability to facilitate a just peace is not a result of simply making a conscious decision to do so. Anyone who wishes to be *effective* as a positive agent for change, who wants to be successful in facilitating *shalom/salaam* in the world, must do the necessary work beforehand. It is not simply a matter of will, but of work. No one ever achieved excellence in music, athletics, or the sciences by just deciding to be really good at it. The actor Will Smith put it well: "Skill is only developed by hours and hours and hours of beating on your craft!" It is no different for those who desire to make the world a more peaceful and just place.

A Place for Cultivation

Unfortunately, we in the West do not often speak of self-cultivation. Even the idea itself can seem foreign to us. While we may exercise to stay physically fit, or read inspiring books, rarely do we hear of people engaging a particular discipline to cultivate virtue within themselves. We generally do not find adults trying to nurture and develop their character. This kind of practice is even uncommon in our religious communities!

We take a different approach, however, with children. Where I live, the great majority of parents sign up their children for baseball, basketball, and/ or soccer. The primary reason we do this is not in the hope that our children will earn a college scholarship or turn professional. It is also not because we simply want our kids to have fun. Rather, what is much more important to us as parents is that our children become physically active, work with a team, develop respect for authorities, and learn how to win and lose graciously. We sign kids up for sports to cultivate their character, develop their bodies, and be part of a social network. Throughout their early years, parents try to find activities for their children that will develop resilience, patience, diligence, and other good habits and character traits.

It is unfortunate that this sensible approach to nurturing our children largely ends when they enter high school. At that point, it seems, we decide their character is largely fixed. Now it is time to prepare them for college or a career by having them do all the right activities and get the right grades. Teenagers no longer play lacrosse in order to cultivate their character.

One notable exception to this is service in the military. Recruits undergo rigorous training to develop not only their bodies and professional skills, but they are forced to mature in many other ways. The image of a directionless teenager heading off to boot camp with shaggy hair, bad posture, and a lack of focus is a common one—as is his return in uniform, looking sharp, self-disciplined, and focused. It is a shame that we tend to limit such life-changing opportunities for personal development to those who enter military service or law enforcement.

Many religious traditions have significant disciplines of self-cultivation, but again, these are rarely emphasized in the West. India is the origin of many of the Eastern traditions, where meditative and physical practices of tremendous depth were created. Shedding our ignorance and illusions, and developing what Gandhi called "soul force" (*satyāgraha*), is not achieved by an act of the will; it is the result of years of effort, spiritual exercise, and deep personal introspection. In China, living in harmony with the *Dao* requires the same commitment to religious discipline. Cultivation of the mind, in Confucianism, to become a "gentleman" (*junzi*), requires tremendous learning, discipline, and ritual practice. Buddhism, likewise, is full of physical and meditative disciplines, from multi-year pilgrimages to thousands of hours spent in meditation. Japanese culture, influenced by Confucianism and Buddhism, still emphasizes the importance of *shugyō*, an austere physical and mental discipline one carries out for decades to cultivate the self. There is no quick and easy shortcut on the way to excellence.

There are indeed some comparable traditions in the West, although they are generally less well-known or discussed. Roman Catholicism, Eastern Orthodoxy, Sufism, and Judaism have meditative disciplines and some acts of physical asceticism (e.g., fasting), designed to deepen the spiritual relationship with God. For example, meditating on the sufferings of Christ while praying the rosary can be a meaningful and effective practice for cultivating gratitude. Protestants, on the other hand, tend to avoid practices of self-development, as they often worry that such focus on the individual detracts from salvation coming from God, given through faith alone. The Protestants have a point here, but it is unfortunate that they have often completely overlooked the values of self-cultivation.[20]

Islam has the principle of *jihad*, which is generally misunderstood by most people today. The word does not mean "holy war," but actually "exertion, striving." In the Koran and early Islam, the word was often associated with the internal struggle to overcome sin. Efforts to overcome that which stands contrary to the will of God (for example, one's pride or greed) are *jihad*. (While this can refer to defensive armed conflict against those who prevent Muslims from living and worshiping in peace, this has been referred to as the "lesser *jihad*."[21])

Many people in both the East and West sincerely desire to create peace and safety in their communities. While that desire is necessary, it is not sufficient. The pacifist John Yoder knew that finding peaceful resolutions to violent situations is not easy. He wrote, "I am still more likely to find [alternatives to lethal force] if I have disciplined my impulsiveness and fostered my creativity by the study and practice of a nonviolent lifestyle."[22] Whether or not one is a pacifist, we must acknowledge that finding the best solutions to (potentially) violent situations requires the best in us. And the best in us is only brought out through hard work and effort.

For those who believe in a just use of violence, there is a danger in seeing violence as the first choice whenever danger arises. Yoder and other pacifists would have us remember that nonviolent responses to situations are usually present, if we have the intelligence, creativity, resourcefulness, and will to find them. Hauerwas points out that, for many of us, "when violence is justified in principle as a necessary strategy for securing justice, it stills the imaginative search for nonviolent ways of resistance to injustice."[23] For those who believe that violence can be morally acceptable, we must remember that the goal of our involvement in a situation should be a greater

---

20. See Mann, "Lutherans in Need of Self-Discipline," 271–79.

21. Today, because of certain Muslim extremist groups and imprecise reporting by the media, most people identify the word with a "holy war" or terrorism.

22. Yoder, *What Would You Do*, 28. Curiously, Yoder suggests the practice of "aikido" here, which he calls "the nonviolent variant of the martial arts." While aikido has strong peace-loving ethics attached to its founding and practice, it is not exactly nonviolent. It exists to one end of the spectrum of martial arts, with regard to force and brutality, but there is no shortage of pain and severity in its original practice.

23. Hauerwas, *Peaceable Kingdom*, 114.

peace, not always victory. Teachers of Okinawan karate often say that the goal of self-defense is not to win, but to not lose. If we are to follow Augustine, attempting to secure peace, repress evil, and support the good, we must recognize that this is not always achieved best through the defeat of others. One's goal should be the safety of the innocent, not necessarily the defeat of the guilty. At times the latter may be required to achieve the former, but not as often as we might imagine or desire. This is difficult work, and requires the best in us—body, mind, and spirit.

Among those who find violence to be an ethical possibility, there is often the desire to learn how to use it. In an effort to ensure one's own safety, and that of others, many people practice physical disciplines like the martial arts or carry a firearm. They want to learn self-defense, or how to "fight." (I am raising my two sons with the skills to physically defend themselves and others.) The proficiency to physically engage another person, in order to prevent oneself or another from being hurt, maimed, or killed, is certainly a positive and useful ability to possess.

However, insofar as one may wish to establish or restore peace in a potentially violent situation, physical skills are not enough. One needs the intellectual skills to recognize dangers and eliminate threats to people in the safest way possible. The use of physical violence is sometimes necessary, but a tremendous number of bad situations can be resolved without it when people have the creative skills to do so. This requires study, intelligence, and thoughtfulness.

I once heard about an elderly woman who was being followed home by a shady-looking fellow. As the man approached, looking like he was about to assault her, she turned to him and asked with a smile, "Don't I know your mother?" Upon hearing her question, the young man mumbled something in his moment of confusion and walked off. Self-defense is not all about physical strength and prowess.

Large numbers of books on martial arts and "practical self-defense" have been published over the past several decades. While their quality varies, most have focused on the physical skills necessary to neutralize an attacker. In more recent years, however, there has been a growing emphasis on understanding self-defense as the ability to forestall or minimize violence. Authors are now moving beyond simple reliance on more punches, kicks, and elbows. They are teaching the psychology of violence and how to minimize it altogether—even before it starts. This more cerebral approach is an important and long-overdue aspect of "self-defense."[24] Peacemakers must develop intellectual skills as well as physical ones.

---

24. At the top of my list are Miller, *Meditations on Violence*, and Kane and Wilder,

What is far less common is material on what we might call the "spiritual" aspects of self-cultivation, as they relate to violence. On the one hand, there are plenty of books on the ethics of just war theory and the subject of peacemaking. These often discuss the history, justification, and real-world applications of war and peace. Many of these are excellent resources on the ethics of violence, especially as they relate to history, ethical theory, and international contexts—nations going to war against other nations.

Much less common in the literature dealing with the ethics of violence are discussions of how to cultivate a spirit that enables *shalom/salaam* in one's own life and community. Few ask, "How can I overcome my own character flaws in order to be a more effective agent in creating peace in my world?" Our own self-importance, greed, and pride are often the biggest enemies of social harmony, yet we rarely speak of them. The cultivation of virtue is necessary if we are to make the best use of our bodies and minds in responding to a world which is often caught up in violence. To know oneself, and how to spiritually nurture oneself, are essential elements in the pursuit of peace. Unfortunately, we generally spend very little time on such topics. If we are to balance the complementary virtues of kindness and courage, gentleness and strength, we cannot simply will them into existence. They require effort, time, energy, and the knowledge of where to look for the help we need for their cultivation.

With this holistic understanding of self-cultivation, we may now consider what is involved with putting it into practice. We often speak of human beings consisting of "body, mind, and spirit." Whether or not this is ontologically true, this tripartite differentiation of the self can be a meaningful way to talk about the whole of our lives. This final part of the book will examine self-cultivation with regard to these three fundamental aspects of personhood. We will consider how we may cultivate our bodies, minds, and spirits in order to become virtuous in thought as well as action.

The Little Black Book of Violence.

CHAPTER 9

Cultivating Body

Besides, it is a disgrace to grow old through sheer carelessness before seeing what manner of man you may become by developing your bodily strength and beauty to their highest limit. But you cannot see that, if you are careless; for it will not come of its own accord.

—SOCRATES

Physical Fitness

Many people today spend significant time strengthening their bodies, from pickup basketball games to yoga. Others go further, training in CrossFit or for Spartan races. For the most part, we do this for reasons of personal benefit. We want to be healthy, feel good, look good, and sometimes we actually enjoy the activity. Rarely, however, do we think of strengthening our bodies for moral reasons. Yet there are multiple ethical motivations for doing so. Parents should take care of their health in order to be part of their children's lives for as long as possible. Spending large amounts of money on medical care for a neglected body means less money to support charities that tend to the world's neediest. Most of us do not think about maintaining our physical health for the sake of being a good employee. However, it follows from the duty to be a good worker that one finds in many ethical frameworks, from biblical precepts[1] to Confucian virtue ethics.[2]

Cultivating the body is also necessary for one to follow the moral imperative to work toward creating *shalom/salaam* in the world. Simple physical fitness is vital. In 2015, my friend Steve was buying coffee when he noticed that a home across the street was on fire. He ran over, found the family inside, and physically assisted the owners' disabled son in leaving the house. He was able to do this because he had the physical strength and health to do so. While this particular situation did not involve violence, it illustrates a point. When responding to emergencies, whether one is rushing to aid others or fleeing danger, greater physical fitness can make oneself and others safer.

This is not to say that everyone should have the physical constitution required to rescue people from burning buildings. Steve is 6'5" and 250 pounds. My wife, who is 4'11", is probably incapable of a similar feat (although I have learned not to underestimate her). The point is not that everyone should achieve a particular standard of physical health; that would be foolish. People have different bodies, opportunities, medical histories, and abilities. However, everyone can work to improve their health, regardless of their starting point and goals.

Consider how fast you can move. Can you sprint one hundred meters in less than fifteen seconds? If so, you are able to outrun the vast majority of people and can therefore more effectively flee danger, which is a very important part of personal safety. Perhaps you are a bit slower than that. However, if you can run out of a building where there is a fire or active shooter, you are making yourself and first responders safer.

Even if your top speed is only a jog, that is better than a walking pace. When I was twelve years old, my father saw me get knocked down and threatened by a couple teenagers from a considerable distance away. As he was in his late fifties, and not particularly aerodynamic, his top speed was not too impressive. However, he immediately ran toward us and arrived before the violence escalated. Jogging is a better top speed than walking. And the ability to walk still makes you and others safer than if you require assistance.

---

1. "Anyone who does not provide for their relatives, and especially for their own household, has denied the faith and is worse than an unbeliever" (1 Tim 5:8). "Whatever you do, work at it with all your heart, as working for the Lord, not for human masters" (Col 3:23).

2. "In serving one's ruler one deals reverently with the tasks involved and makes the livelihood involved a secondary consideration" (*Analects* 15:38).

To be clear, there is no correlation between speed and virtue. We do not blame people for something they are incapable of doing. If you do not have the potential to carry someone out of a burning building, no one will blame you if you don't. However, most people can make progress. If that involves increasing one's maximum speed from a walk to a jog, then the world is a better place. The person who makes that effort is to be commended. As Dr. Martin Luther King Jr. told the graduating class at Glenville High School, "And so, if you can't fly, run. If you can't run, walk. If you can't walk, crawl. But by all means, keep moving."[3] This is true both metaphorically and literally.

I am always more impressed by the character of the overweight person huffing and puffing on the treadmill, working to improve her health, than the lithe teenager who can effortlessly run up and down the basketball court. The morality is found in the effort, not the ability. Rarely will someone say so publicly, but failure to take care of your body—whether through lack of exercise, poor diet, or drug and alcohol abuse—is a moral decision. Moreover, it is one that affects not only your own well-being, but also that of the people around you.

Self-Defense

As with physical fitness, many people learn self-defense for personal gratification. They want to know how to protect themselves, get in shape, be part of a community, or learn an art form. This is all well and good, but it is possible to view self-defense as an ethical act as well, learning to keep oneself and others safe for the well-being of the community. As we see in cases of international conflict, weakness can invite aggression that may lead to war. What is true of nations also applies to individuals. Strength is an asset that can be used to establish peace. At the same time, learning self-defense requires that one should seriously consider the moral dimensions of what is being practiced. There are both virtues and vices that can be cultivated while training for violence.

It's Not About Winning

Most people think about a martial artist using her knowledge and skill to thrash bad guys. I suspect that most people who join a local club or school have this in mind, at least to some degree. As I did many years ago, people

---

3. King, April 26, 1967. King is citing Langston Hughes.

want to learn how to fight in order to take down those who might oppose them. While such skills are part of many martial arts programs, we hope that practitioners will develop a more mature attitude toward violence and self-defense as they spend more time in the arts. Again, some—but certainly not all—will realize that the goal is not to win, but rather not to lose.[4]

Risuke Otake, a senior teacher of classical Japanese martial arts,[5] writes, "Genuine classical martial studies go hand-in-hand with humane conduct and inculcate a deeply developed moral sense in their exponents. It is not the physical victory that must be fought and won. The true victory is that one is able to obtain his aim without resorting to combat."[6] In the story of Itosu in chapter 8, we saw a martial arts master who demonstrated this ideal. Not only did he keep himself uninjured, but he kept his young assailant free of injury as well. He even managed to open a dialogue with his enemy—a remarkable ending to what began as a physical assault.

The goal of a truly great martial artist, then, is to resolve a situation before violence becomes necessary. Unfortunately, most of us do not have the skillset of Itosu. However, one need not be at his level to follow this principle. Several years ago I was walking through a sketchy part of Manila at night alone. A group of four people—two men and two women—quickly walked up and surrounded me, in an attempted strong-arm robbery.[7] Before their little circle closed around me, I was able to quickly shoot between two of them and turn 180 degrees to face all of them at once. With their primary advantage negated, and with some posturing on my part, I was able to create some additional space between us before I quickly left the scene. The footwork I used was based on the movements of a karate *kata* (form) I have practiced countless times.[8] In this particular case, the use of punches, kicks, or throws was not only unnecessary, but attempting them would have been foolish. I went home uninjured, if a bit shaken; they went home unharmed, and their attempt at unjust gain went unrewarded. This incident did not

4. This is an important principle that comes from Okinawan teachers of karate-do. As discussed above, law enforcement personnel, however, are in a different situation. They cannot flee trouble. They are required to handle and resolve criminal situations, which often means "winning" an altercation. Simply ensuring their own safety is not sufficient, as they are responsible for others.

5. Otake is the current *shihan* of the *Tenshin Shōden Katori Shintō-ryū*.

6. Otake, *Deity and the Sword*. As in Amdur, *Old School*, 46.

7. It is likely that one or more of them were actually armed, but no weapon was brandished during our encounter.

8. Since I do not recall if the turn I made was to the left or right, I cannot say if it was from the final movement of *saifa* or *shisochin kata* I was using. Either way, it had been grooved deeply in my muscle memory and proved reliable.

play out like it would have in the movies. My misadventure was much less entertaining, but it was also much more of a true victory.

Cultivation of Character

When it comes to the practice of self-defense and the cultivation of virtue, there is nothing magical or mystical about training in martial arts that engenders moral development. Moreover, it would be naïve to think that the majority of martial artists think much at all about the moral dimensions of the violence they are learning; quite the opposite, I would expect. However, in the martial traditions of many cultures—not least Otake's Japan—there are resources and traditions in place to direct students in the direction of ethical cultivation. It is a question of who will avail themselves of these.

Aikido is one example of a modern martial art that features a very strong ethic in its curriculum, as the founder wanted to see his art used to create peace between peoples and nations, not more fighting. While some believe that aikido is nonviolent,[9] that is an overly-romantic notion. Still, ethics is part of the ethos of aikido. Ellis Amdur, a longtime practitioner of this art, explains the goal of training: "Aikidō is training in reconciliation— in the ability to step into a conflicted situation and effect *the most peaceful resolution that is possible under the circumstances*, and martial effectiveness is regarded as a means to that end, not an end in itself."[10] Sometimes events can be managed with complete nonviolence. Other times, that luxury does not exist.

The cultivation of virtue, then, is not about a rejection of all violence. What is virtuous is the genuine desire to use as little violence as necessary within a "conflicted situation." A Filipino friend, who also happens to be a Roman Catholic priest, spent years studying aikido. During one of his trips to Africa, he was forced to make use of this skill to actually hurt someone. In the city where he was living and working with the poor, young men would often attempt to pickpocket people. However, in doing so, they were not just interested in procuring a single item; they were attempting to gauge the response of the victim. They wanted to see if the person would fight back or just allow himself to be victimized. If the latter, they would then return and take more and more from that individual. My friend explained that if you did not want to be assaulted and robbed of all your possessions, you needed to respond forcefully to the first attempt. He then demonstrated for me how he grabbed one young man by the hand, performing an impressive

9. Yoder, *What Would You Do*, 28.
10. Amdur, *Dueling with O'Sensei*, 234. Emphasis mine.

single-handed inside-wrist-lock (*kote gaeshi*) that made me yelp. In this context, that was the most peaceful resolution he could achieve. Without that skill, greater violence and harm would likely have been the result.

What Do I Really Know?

Beyond the challenge of using the minimal force necessary, martial artists must also know what skills they truly have, and in what circumstances they will work. While many people study various martial arts around the world today, and work on all sorts of "techniques" for fighting, one of the biggest challenges for the practitioner is to be honest with himself about what he actually knows and what he can actually do. Delusion is ever-present in the martial arts world. Many people believe they possess self-defense skills, but really have little more than the ability to play fight games in the completely safe environment of their dojo. Their joint locks and throws work only on compliant partners. Sparring is about tagging the other person before they are tagged. Their movements lack power, balance, and precision. I have seen too many martial artists completely befuddled when someone steps on their foot and shoves them to the ground in a non-scripted situation.

Unfortunately, it is very difficult for us to know how we would actually react in a violent encounter. How effective would our skills actually turn out to be? Every practitioner of martial arts must constantly engage in critical assessment of this question. They must constantly think about and test the effectiveness of what they know and can actually do. "Could I effectively do this against someone who has fifty pounds more muscle than I do, is faster than I am, and is really, really angry? Would my reverse punch really stop that person cold?" That can be a good place to start. Confidence is, in general, a positive thing. Confidence can defuse dangerous situations. However, misplaced confidence can also be disastrous.

In addition to knowing one's actual facility with self-defense, practitioners should also be honest about which contexts they are training for. Training for competition in Tae Kwon Do is great, as long as you realize that you are not preparing for barroom brawls where there is little room to maneuver, the floor is wet and slippery, and an angry biker is holding a broken beer bottle right at the level you normally kick. Being a great wrestler is wonderful and practical, unless you are facing multiple attackers—one of whom is going to kick you in the head with her boots if you end up grappling on the floor. Muay Thai is a brutally effective art, but not the best resource if you are working in law enforcement and need to restrain people, rather than split their faces open with an elbow.

Every art has strengths and liabilities; this is not a question of better and worse. The key is to know what you can and cannot do. In recent years, my karate class has had a significant number of young women as students. In terms of self-defense, what I focus on is mostly social violence. If a drunk or angry person comes up and grabs one of my students by the wrists, pushes her against the wall, grabs her hair, or takes a big swing at her head, she has been trained to deal with that. She is not trained to deal with a skilled knife-fighter. The skills most of my students pick up in a few years are not focused on responding to an asocial encounter where a predator approaches with a gun and tries to kidnap her. Some of that is discussed, but that is not our focus. No class can do everything. It is important to be knowledgeable about different kinds of violence, as well as one's actual ability to respond to them. Ignorance and false confidence can put people in very bad situations.

Breadth and Depth

No martial art, even the eclectic ones that seek the "best of all, worst of none," will develop effective skills for all possible situations. Martial arts, from krav maga to hapkido, are all developed for specific contexts, not all possible ones. The skills that a Marine needs in Afghanistan are going to be different than what I want in rural Pennsylvania. Nevertheless, there are ethical and practical advantages in developing breadth in one's knowledge of self-defense. It simply allows more options in seeking the most peaceful resolution that is possible under the circumstances.

Years ago, I met a boy who practiced a traditional style of karate. He was excellent! Perhaps the best I have ever seen at his age. This style of karate, however, is all about punching and kicking. As a result, his striking was superb. Unfortunately, that was just about the full extent of his skillset. He could block, punch, and kick. One day, he got in an altercation at school with another boy who was not a martial artist. When words turned to actions, he responded with the only tool in his toolbox; he punched the other kid in the chest. Regrettably, he hit the other boy so hard he put him in the hospital. While I do not know the particulars of the situation, I have often found myself thinking that with his natural ability and years of training, it is unfortunate that he did not learn the skills necessary to control another person without injuring him. It is not my intention to critique the training that he received, but I do believe that a wider breadth of self-defense knowledge would have served everyone in that situation much better.

Most of the time, defeating a violent adversary requires the use of even greater violence. In discussing the realities of warfare, Michael Walzer points to the sad reality that when nations take up arms against each other—the violence must be escalated for one side to win. "Here is the ultimate tyranny: those who resist aggression are forced to imitate, and perhaps even to exceed, the brutality of the aggressor."[11] Whatever level of force is used by a belligerent, those defending against it must usually respond with at least as much force. This, however, need not always be the case. In many circumstances, a broader range of options and abilities allows for the use of less violence.

There are numerous examples in modern warfare where superior resources mean less violence was required. Precision strikes allow one side to engage the enemy with far less brutality than is directed at them or their allies. Nations with a greater arsenal and technology can choose less violence in their attacks on the enemy. With reference to *jus in bello*, their actions can address the requirement of "due care" much more easily. They have a breadth of options which allows for the possibility of less forcefulness and bloodshed.

The same is true in the realm of civilian self-defense. The greater one's "arsenal," the more opportunities one has to choose a less violent response to a dangerous situation. Hapkido is a Korean martial art that combines striking, throwing, and grappling. Its curriculum is more comprehensive than its cousin taekwondo. As a result, hapkido practitioners can develop the ability to respond to violent threats with a greater variety of defenses. Dick Morgan, a senior practitioner of this art, explains, "As the practitioner becomes more and more advanced, contact with the attacker becomes less violent, less forceful, less necessary. And thus, at the master level, hapkido and aikidō tend to greatly resemble one another."[12] The greater the skill, the less force is necessary.

When I was a teenager, I was attacked by a very angry individual with a knife. Fortunately, he was only seven years old. Needless to say, my response was gentle. I controlled his arm, removed the knife, and put him in his room. No violence was necessary, just a bit of physical force. I was able to do this because, compared to him, I was far stronger and easily able to defend myself. Imagine having the same relative advantage to someone your own size and strength. In that case, if assaulted, your response could be far less violent to assure your own safety than if you had no such skill. Again, the greater the skill, the less force is necessary. Of course, the only way to acquire such skill is through years and years, if not decades, of dedicated

11. Walzer, *Just and Unjust Wars*, 32.
12. As in Amdur, *Dueling with O'Sensei*, 114.

training. Thus, by training in the use of violence, we develop the physical capacity to resolve conflicts with less violence.

In military, law enforcement, and civilian contexts, this can even lead to the point where projected strength prevents violence from erupting in the first place. Most people do not want to run afoul of a nation with precision smart bombs and the will to use them. The presence of a police officer, with a pistol and radio to call for backup, will give most people pause if they are planning some illegal shenanigans. The same applies with people who are able to project a strength that comes from physical training. I am not referring to the guy who wears a "Joe's Karate Dojo" or "Tapout" T-shirt to the mall. Rather, it is the quiet strength, confidence, and competence that comes with many years of hard work. This has the potential to stop fights before they begin. Hayward Nishioka, who was in more than his fair share of scuffles as a teenager, relates the following story: "The funniest thing was that, as I was learning judo, I used it on maybe half a dozen occasions . . . After I started using judo to defend myself, I found that some people were afraid of me. As I got better, my aura [of confidence] defended me, and I didn't have to fight as much."[13]

This ability to forestall violence is not simply about reputation, muscular development, or mystical aura. A combination of factors, many of which may be subconscious, can combine to project a strength that thwarts aggression. Franz Bork, a well-known German karate practitioner (1939–2012), taught this: "Therefore it is best to prevent aggressive situations as early as possible. Karate offers many options for this to the student, like awareness of one's surroundings (*zanshin*), a calm, immovable mind even under great pressure (*fudoshin*) or a self-confident posture (*kamae*). Understood and practiced like this, karate can actually help prevent violence."[14]

Those with strength and skill have a resource for maintaining peace, not just restoring it. This is an asset generally unavailable to those who have not put in the work. In the words of Martin Luther, "[O]ne sword keeps the other in the scabbard."[15] (Ironically, Luther had no skill with a sword. In fact, he almost killed himself with one when he accidentally cut his own leg open and nearly bled to death.)

---

13. Young, "Hayward Nishioka," para. 9.
14. Golinski, "Conversations with Franz Bork," 58.
15. Luther, "Whether Soldiers, Too, Can be Saved," 122.

Hazards

If there are multiple ways in which training in the martial arts can enable one as a peacemaker, there are quite a number of dangers as well. There is nothing mystical or special about martial arts that transforms its practitioners into warrior-sages. In fact, there are elements of martial arts practice that can contribute to behaviors that are brutish and manipulative. Individual practitioners must be vigilant in their self-analysis. Instructors must keep a double watch, as they are also responsible for those who they teach. According to Kanryo Higaonna (1853–1915), "Teaching a martial art is like handing out a weapon. Handing that weapon to the wrong person can be dangerous and could result in the death of innocent people."[16]

It is not only sociopaths and mentally unstable students who pose a danger. Most human beings have inclinations that can be distorted by power. In the case of martial arts, the acquired power can be intoxicating. When a 170-pound middle-aged guy can overcome a noncompliant three-hundred-pound man, the effect is exhilarating. When a woman can strike a larger man at will, while the man cannot even seem to touch her, it can do significant things to her ego. This effect may then be magnified by others in the room who voice their admiration and amazement, bow to the skilled individuals, and refer to them with lofty titles. In such a context, there resides the potential for both considerable good and considerable harm. Power can serve a great good; it can also corrupt. The direction is determined by the individual, not the art.

Martial artist, Marine veteran, and clinical psychologist Richard Heckler describes the natural affinity for physical power and dominance that many people have. "This urgent call of nature longs to be tested, seeks to be challenged beyond itself. The warrior within us beseeches Mars, the god of War, to deliver us to that crucial battlefield that will redeem us into the terrifying immediacy of the moment. We want to face our Goliath so we may be reminded that the warrior David is alive, in us . . . We long for the encounter that will ultimately empower us with dignity and honor."[17] This power is felt (and enjoyed!) most acutely in dominating others, and for many people it can lead to the desire to approach all situations as opportunities to dominate. Rather than seek the best options to minimize violence and create *shalom/salaam*, we want to play the hero who steps in to save the day by vanquishing the enemy. It feels good and looks good, but it can create great harm. The person in love with his own power may have a hard

---

16. Higaonna, *History of Karate*, 49.

17. Heckler, *In Search of the Warrior Spirit*; cited in Grossman, *On Killing*, 184.

time seeking resolutions that require him to lose face. Saying "I'm sorry, it's my fault" is often the best response to situations of social violence, but those words may get caught in the throat of the person in love with his own heroism and ability.

If one has the ability to resolve dangerous situations with violence, it is easy to fool oneself into thinking that doing so is always the best option. The fact is, our human reason serves our selfish desires more often than we care to admit.[18] The advantage of the pacifist, as we have seen, is that she knows she must think critically and creatively to find the best solution. Those with the power to fight (and the belief that violence may be justified) are more likely to do so even when other better options may be available.

Unfortunately, the temptation to use violence is not so unusual. Even those of us who genuinely want to avoid violence can find ourselves attracted by its siren song. Eminent scholar of Buddhism Paul Demiéville (1894–1979) noted that even Buddhists are susceptible to this. Even those who abjure and reject violence can find ways to justify it. If an action feels good, we will do what we want and offer justifications later.

> Men are made in such a way that they need reasons to justify bending their principles. Consequently, when they eschew a bad habit, it too often comes back, masked as a virtue. Buddhists have taken many alternative routes trying their utmost to legitimize many habits that run completely counter to the Buddhist precept of no-killing.[19]

The martial artist may pay lip service to the importance of not fighting unless it is "absolutely necessary," but still end up fighting with regularity. In each situation he encounters, he decides it is, in fact, necessary.

I recently watched a video where a staged bullying situation among teenagers was playing out in a fast-food restaurant. The implied question was this: "Would you step in and help?" Of course, I was sure that I would impose myself and talk down the aggressors through a show of strength and machismo. However, when I watched a young woman handle the situation by walking over to the table with her tray, sit down with the bullied boy, introduce herself to his tormentor, shake his hand, and then proceed with a firm but polite conversation, I was really impressed, and a bit embarrassed. There was not the slightest hint of the potential for violence, and yet the situation was resolved extraordinarily.

I have argued that there is nothing special about the study of martial arts practice that makes a person more virtuous or enlightened. At the

18. Mann, "Luther on Reason," 1–17.
19. Demiéville, "Buddhism and War," 38.

same time, training in fighting disciplines that are more closely connected to their original purposes can force moral questions on the practitioner. That is to say, if you are practicing an art in which the consideration of life and death, of killing or maiming another human being, is ever-present, then the seriousness of your actions may be more strongly impressed upon you. Hopefully, this forces one to consider ethical questions about the nature of the discipline. Training in acts of brutality can and should prompt moral deliberation. Unfortunately, this is generally not the case. In my early years training in martial arts, techniques that were vicious, lethal, or "traditional," prompted thoughts of how "cool" they were, rather than serious deliberation on the nature of what I was learning. Eventually, I started facing the ethical questions more squarely.

The more we remove martial arts from their original contexts, however, the more they can become playthings that do not merit serious introspection. In discussing the classical Japanese martial tradition of the *naginata* (i.e., the glaive), Amdur shares his concern about modern competitive appropriations (*atarashi naginata*) of this traditional discipline. "By removing the considerations of one's own death and one's responsibility for the other's fate, atarashi naginata may have removed one of the major impetuses for the development of an ethical stance. All that may remain for many trainees is a sport with the emphasis on winning or losing a match."[20]

Today, martial arts are heavily oriented toward sport. Judo, wrestling, taekwondo, boxing, and now karate are all in the Olympics. While this has its benefits, it also creates attitudes regarding the practice of violence that are not helpful. First of all, sport obviously requires the use of techniques that are relatively safe. Whether full-contact or point-sparring, grappling or throwing, sporting events take place under direct supervision of qualified people. No one is too worried about being killed. Serious injuries can take place, but this is true in many other sports as varied as rugby and cheerleading. (In fact, martial arts competitions are generally much safer than either of those.) As a result, people do not think too much about the brutality of fighting. In a competition, a person may get knocked out and fall down on a padded surface. The fight will immediately stop and medical professionals will attend to the person. In real violence, the victim falls and hits her head on concrete and may continue to be kicked and stomped repeatedly, after which she may simply be left lying on the ground with no one to attend to her. Sport-fighting creates an illusion that violence is safer than it really is.

In addition to the misperception of the true nature of violence, sport fosters and encourages a strong desire to defeat others. By no means am

20. Amdur, *Old School*, 216.

I opposed to sport. In fact, I support and still participate in martial arts competitions. However, one must be aware that the overwhelming desire to "win" in violence can be ethically problematic. As discussed above, the goal in a violent encounter should not be to win, but not to lose. Running away, apologizing, redirecting the conversation, attempting as little force as possible, none of these fit in a sport environment. When martial arts training revolves completely around competition, everything is oriented toward winning, and winning big. Such athletes are likely to have only one goal in mind, then, if they encounter an aggressor. This is unhealthy and imprudent.

In 1942, Ueshiba wrote, "The Way of the warrior has been misunderstood as a means to kill and destroy others. Those who seek competition are making a grave mistake. To smash, injure, or destroy is the worst sin a human being can commit. The real way of a warrior is to prevent slaughter—it is the art of peace, the power of love."[21] Not surprisingly, aikido has largely eschewed competition. In doing so, it believes itself to be holding more firmly to the teaching of its founder.[22] However, this lack of competition—working against non-compliant partners who want to defeat you—has often been cited as a reason that aikido may lack real world effectiveness. Competition can be one very helpful aspect of martial arts training. I believe, in fact, that it is necessary for one to develop legitimate skills of self-defense. However, when the entire art becomes a combat sport, there is a real ethical danger.[23]

21. As in Raposa, *Meditation and the Martial Arts*, 9.

22. In other Japanese martial arts, like judo and Shotokan karate, the desires of their founders to minimize competition were promptly ignored upon their passing, so that today these are among the most sport-oriented martial arts.

23. See Mann, *When Buddhists Attack*, 183–200.

CHAPTER 10

Cultivating Mind

[A]s a field, though fertile, cannot yield a harvest without cultivation, no more
can the mind without learning; thus each is feeble without the other.

—CICERO

For those who desire to work for peace and stand up against injustice,
broad shoulders and a crisp left hook are not enough. In fact, very rarely
are they necessary. As the pacifists remind us, we can regularly forestall
violence with enough thought and creativity. Violence is not necessary to
stop violence nearly as often as we think it is. We can often come up with
better solutions. However, whether a situation requires the use of violence
or not, Reinhold Niebuhr was right: "Critical intelligence is a prerequisite
of justice."[1]

At the international level, nations benefit not only by having the resources to defend themselves and their allies, but by knowing when and how
to use them. It is not enough to identify both a just cause and just means, but
"securing peace . . . repressing the evil and supporting the good" demands
tremendous depth in understanding diplomacy, economics, cultural history, religion, and battlefield tactics—to name just a few. For citizens who
participate in their democracies, it requires them to be well-educated and
well-read when they vote and advocate for various public policies.

On the level of an individual who may face violence in her community,
which is our primary concern in this chapter, critical intelligence is just as

1. Niebuhr, *Interpretation of Christian Ethics*, 100.

important. The subject matter may differ, but knowledge, insight, and cleverness are necessary if one is to perceive violence correctly and respond to it effectively. As with the training of the body, this simply requires putting in the work.

Understanding Violence

I recently began a self-defense seminar I was teaching by saying, "If all you know about violence is what you have seen in movies and on TV, then please recognize that you know nothing about violence." It is, after all, better to know that you know nothing, than to think you know something when you don't. If we, as morally responsible citizens, are to deal with situations of possible violence in effective ways, we must first know something about the nature of violence.

When I first began training in martial arts, I was under the mistaken impression that real violence was similar to the sparring we did in class. The only difference, I thought, was that we would not pull our punches in real life. Looking back, I find my ignorance at that time rather embarrassing. In the dojo, two people get ready to fight and begin at the same time. The room is cleared of dangerous objects, everything is well lit, and no one grabs a weapon. None of the people watching from the sidelines suddenly jump on your back and start pulling your hair. Most importantly, someone watches over the "fight" and stops it immediately if someone gets hurt. While sparring is an important aspect of training in self-defense, it is very different from violence in the real world. Not understanding actual violence makes us far less effective in keeping ourselves and others safe. In fact, being well informed about the nature of violence is more valuable than being the most skilled fighter at your local martial arts school. If you want to minimize violence in your world, you must study the nature of violence.

To begin with, it is essential to understand that there are different types of violence. For example, being able to differentiate social from asocial violence is not about an interesting psychological analysis of the perpetrator; it is imperative to keep oneself safe. In a situation of social violence, where a bully is posturing in front of his friends, appeasing him and apologizing may be the best approach. In a situation of asocial violence, where a predator is trying to get you into his vehicle so he can drive you to a secluded place, assault, and kill you, appeasement is very wrong. Your own conditioned politeness and decency are used against you.

In social violence, there are certain rules that are more likely to be followed. You are unlikely to be stabbed and stuffed in a trunk because you "was lookin' at my girl." In asocial violence, such extreme and violent actions can follow after such a statement as "Excuse me, do you have the time?" A predator is not looking for a fight. Miller explains, "In predatory violence, the victim is a resource. The attack is a planned, efficient, and safe way for the attacker to get what he wants from that resource. It is not a contest. It is not a fight. It looks and feels nothing like competition at any level."[2] Martial artists too often think of violence resembling the situation where two individuals face off against each other, put up their defenses, and begin simultaneously. Such ignorance is very dangerous.

Being knowledgeable about violence means, for example, knowing that predatory assaults by men against women may happen like this: "The victim was approached from the rear/side/front, a threat was made with a weapon, and then the weapon was hidden. Then the victim's right upper arm was held by the attacker's left hand and the victim was led away."[3] Being informed means knowing that a person taken to a secondary location in a scenario like this is probably not coming back. Being educated means knowing how to observe one's environment effectively and spot a threat before the actual danger presents itself. Most importantly, cultivating the mind means practicing awareness and the mental preparation that might be necessary to avoid, flee, or fight out of such a situation. Remember, it is not about winning, but about not losing.

This book is not the place to learn all about different types of violence and how best to respond to them. I have previously cited authors like Miller, Wilder, and Kane whose books are a tremendous resource for those desiring to understand the nature of violence. Some of these more recent books are even more useful because of their suggestions regarding how to practice the principles they teach.[4] We need to move beyond self-defense "techniques" where "Attacker grabs Victim by his lapels and Victim performs the following actions to defeat Attacker." Rather, we must study ways of training ourselves to spot potential violence, understand it, avoid it, defuse it, and survive it. Moreover, it is not enough to store information somewhere in your brain. We must have it grooved in, so that proper responses will happen quickly and easily without conscious deliberation. In a bone-chilling assault, there is no time to try and remember what you read in a book on the subject last year.

2. Miller, *Meditations on Violence*, 52.
3. Nash, "Condition Black," as cited in Miller, *Meditations on Violence*, 53.
4. E.g., Miller, *Training for Sudden Violence*.

Knowing Oneself

As discussed above, an important part of mental cultivation is understanding the different forms that violence can take, as well as what responses are helpful for different situations. It is also very important to know yourself and your own potential. What are you physically able to do? What are you psychologically able to carry out? What ethical lines will you not cross? Knowing the answers to these questions is essential before things go all cattywumpus. One should not wait and find out in the midst of a life-threatening encounter. The advice of the Oracle at Delphi rings true again: "Know thyself."

Physical Ability

In 2014, the satirical website *The Onion* posted a video reporting on a study that showed, "Average Male 4,000% Less Effective in Fights Than They Imagine." The piece features a spokesperson from the Department of Health and Human Services describing the details of the study, interspersed with young men who voiced their groundless braggadocio about what they would do in a fight. One skinny guy, whose physical demonstrations of fighting betrayed his utter lack of ability, explained:

> If some guy ever came at me, and I needed to take him down quick, I'd just disorient him with a quick blow to the face and then I'd knee him in the gut. The trick is to just keep your fists real tight and punch with your knuckles if you really want to f*** somebody up. I mean, you hope it doesn't come to the point where you have to grab a barstool and smash it over somebody's head, but if he's being a real d***, and you need to draw a little blood, you really don't have a choice.[5]

As with most humor, there is more than a grain of truth to this. Guys with no training are often sure they can fight and beat other guys. I did when I was a boy, until the neighbor kid down the street helped me to see things differently. The point is not that people without training should never raise their hands to defend themselves, but they should be honest with themselves about their complete lack of skill.

Of course, it is not just untrained people who are delusional. In my experience, the majority of martial artists are mistaken about how effective their abilities would be in a genuinely violent altercation. This book

---

5. "Report: Average Male," 0:47–1:09.

is not the place to break down all the issues and problems with training self-defense. However, a critical thinker should be able to differentiate most martial arts training from real-world violence. In a martial arts school, there is always someone there to stop things if problems arise, and we know it. No one there ever picks up a two-by-four, screams that they are going to smash your face in, and charges at you with the intent to do so. People must constantly engage in critical self-assessment of their training and their abilities. As discussed above, confidence is good, but misplaced confidence can get you killed.

A few years ago I visited a local MMA[6] gym with a reputation for being pretty rough. On one of my first nights there, I was sparring a guy who forcefully snatched my head down and put me in a position known as a Standing Guillotine. I had been in this position before, and so I calmly started setting up the counter. However, before I could begin, he forcefully yanked me up in the air so that I was dangling by my neck. As I tapped out, it suddenly occurred to me that my regular training partners worked at a more moderate and considerate pace. This guy was stronger and more competitive than most people I had trained with, and I learned something very valuable: my skillset had a serious hole in it. By not having an accurate understanding of how my own abilities measured up against others, I was less safe than I thought. This false self-assessment could have proven disastrous in another context.[7] Such experiences are frustrating, but they should actually be welcomed.

It is impossible to know exactly how well we might perform in all situations, or what our breaking point is. However, martial artists should always seek greater critical intelligence of their actual abilities. The more we learn about ourselves, what we can and cannot do, the safer we make ourselves and others. When should I run? When should I stand and fight? How should I fight? Knowledge of one's physical abilities is essential to answering such questions. We never reach perfect self-knowledge, but we must constantly strive to reach a better understanding of who we are.

Psychology

Knowledge of your physical abilities is vital, but no less important is the awareness of what your mind will let you do. As discussed in chapter 7, many women talk about carrying their car keys between their knuckles, so

---

6. MMA stands for "Mixed Martial Arts."

7. Subsequently, I worked out a better defense to such a heavy-handed Standing Guillotine, and no one has caught me with it again—at least at the time of this writing.

they can attack the eyes of an assailant. While this might be an effective thing to do in some circumstances, the vast majority of people cannot take a sharp piece of metal and ram it into the soft sphere of a human eyeball. Our natural resistance to such acts of brutality is, generally speaking, a good thing. So, if you are not capable of such an act, don't carry your keys that way! Doing so gives a false sense of confidence. A hesitating or weak response, if a threat actually presents itself, can increase the level of violence directed at the victim. If you cannot gouge an eyeball with a key, that's fine. Just admit it to yourself. Knowledge of your own psychology keeps you and others safer.

I have been learning a bit of Filipino martial arts for a number of years. This art often involves the use of a knife to defend oneself. In many cases, specific sequences end with the practitioner using the knife to slice or stab the other person. I have practiced these dutifully for years, with the same enthusiasm of a person learning the art of fencing. In other words, while I logically know what is being simulated, I am generally disconnected from any existential sense of what I am practicing. The question that demands an answer is this: could I really stab another person in the liver repeatedly, or cut into someone's neck to rip open his carotid artery? I honestly do not know, and hope I never find out. However, not knowing the answer is a liability to my own safety. As others have suggested, if you could not go to a pig farm and cut the throat and kill a living sow (with permission from the owner, of course), then why do you think you could cut open another human being? Perfect self-knowledge may escape us, but we should get to know ourselves as well as possible.

Ethics

In addition to knowing your physical and psychological potential, it is also important to know your ethical convictions before things turn sideways. While there is considerable overlap between what your "mind" will allow you to do and what your ethics will permit, they are distinct. On the one hand, your own moral code may say that killing in self-defense is acceptable, but you may not be able to pull the trigger. On the other, there may be actions that you could do—you might even want to do!—but your conscience insists that they are wrong and should not be carried out.

One of the most important lessons I have learned after teaching ethics for nearly two decades, and attempting to live virtuously myself, is that we should be clear with ourselves about our ethical principles before we encounter the messiness of life. What moral lines will you not cross? If you are suddenly asked to break a safety rule on a construction site to save money for your boss, it is helpful if you have worked out your convictions beforehand. You do not want to be standing there, tools in hand, considering one of the most important decisions of your life for the first time. Today, more than ever, we need to have our moral principles worked out beforehand. In the business world, you may be asked to do something morally ambiguous or tempting. Previous generations had time to think through the situation before they typed up a letter and mailed it, or made changes in a ledger. Today, people expect an immediate decision on e-mail or Skype. There is less time to ruminate. We need to know our ethical principles beforehand.

This is exponentially more important in acts of violence, where you may have less than a second to determine whether an act is morally right or not. Here, the stakes may be your own life or the lives of others. While there are no guarantees that we will always get it right, even with the best of intentions, knowing your own ethical convictions before you are forced to act is of paramount importance. This serves three important functions:

1. You are more likely to act well if you have thought through what is acceptable and what is not.

2. You will be better able to deal with the psychological consequences if you acted with pre-established ethics, rather than trying to justify your behaviors after the fact.

3. That moment of ethical cogitation, which you should have worked out beforehand, could make the difference between someone living and someone dying. For those working in the military or law enforcement, this possibility is very real. For the rest of us, we pray we will never face such a situation, but there are no guarantees.

Rory Miller discusses ethical hesitation, with the clear, direct, and honest tone necessary in such considerations. I quote him at length here:

> These hesitations are what I call glitches, the things that might make you freeze in a survival situation. They indicate that you have moral and ethical issues with using force. Congratulations. We all do. But it's a damn good idea to know what they are before someone tries to kill you.
>
> When you find your glitches, don't try to fix them or judge them. Not yet. Just bring them out into the light and examine them.
>
> So, same basic scenario: someone coming at you with a lethal weapon, a fourteen-inch butcher knife. The threat wants to

kill you, and you are concerned but armed. Do you shoot? Do you feel OK with it? What if . . .

- the threat is fourteen years old? Twelve? Ten? Six?

- the threat is a woman?

- a pregnant woman?

- your children are watching?

- the threat's children are watching?

- it is someone you love, like a veteran father having a flash-back, or your own child suffering from an acute psychotic episode?

- you are being filmed by a news crew?

- the threat is severely developmentally disabled, incapable of knowing what he or she is doing?[8]

Miller's examples combine both ethical and psychological consider-ations. If we are honest, most of us are not ready to give a quick and un-equivocal response to all these questions. However, it should be clear that struggling with them and coming to a clearer understanding of ourselves and our moral convictions is of tremendous importance and value for mak-ing good ethical decisions.

Cultivating Skills to Avoid Violence

As I have argued before, there are numerous alternatives to the use of violence for those with the will and creativity to find them. The question, however, is whether we actually practice creating them. There may be plenty of alternatives to fighting, but will you suddenly recognize them in that moment? Probably not. As with training the body, it is necessary to spend time developing the ability to forestall violence as well. The person who says there are always alternatives to fighting but has not spent considerable time working through them in her mind actually has very few options.

Imagine driving into the parking lot of your local grocery store one evening and seeing an intoxicated young man harassing a young woman in a hijab. The woman looks frightened, not knowing what to do. Go! You might sit in your car for a while and work through your options. That might even be the best thing to do at that moment, but every second you do not act could mean she is one second closer to being assaulted. It means one second

---

8. Miller, *Training for Sudden Violence,* 116.

longer before the police arrive, if you decide to call them. As you sit and think through your options, because you never previously worked through such a scenario, you need to ask some really important questions:

Do I approach them? Does this merit a call to 911? Should I go inside first and find a store employee?

If I approach them, do I first grab a weapon out of the car? What can I use? What are the legal implications of doing so? Do I brandish it or hide it? And would it be just a bluff? Can I calm down a situation while standing there with a tire-iron in my hand? Might that prompt him to pull a gun if he has one? If the police show up and I'm standing there with a weapon, might I be mistaken for the bad guy? What bad things could follow from that?

If I approach them only to talk, do I talk to him or her? Do I scold him or try to find common ground? Do I pretend to be lost and ask for directions, just to change the narrative and ratchet down the hostility? What exactly would I say? Do I tell them they are being filmed on the store's security cameras? Where do I hold my hands?

If it comes to violence, can I see if he is carrying a weapon? Is he wearing a jacket over a holster? Is that a pocketknife in his front pocket? Does he look physically strong? Does he look capable of fighting? Which approaches to fighting work best on someone intoxicated? Which do not?

What exactly is this situation? Is he a bigot harassing a Muslim? Is he an acquaintance? brother? husband? Do I remember correctly that inserting yourself into a domestic dispute is one of the dumbest things you can do?

Fortunately we have brains that can process a great deal of material quite quickly, but that is still a lot to ponder. Furthermore, sometimes the best solution to a problem does not occur to you until an hour later—or the next day. (How often do you come up with the best witty comeback at just the right moment?) Making these decisions in the moment is not the way to come up with the optimal solution to a problem. The less time you have to think, the less clearly you will be thinking. Moreover, the best ideas often come after a period of rumination. If, on the other hand, you have worked out a number of answers to such questions beforehand, you will have fewer variables to consider in the moment and can think through them more clearly. You will have better options.

The bad news is that doing all of this requires work; the good news is that it can be fun. Instead of immediately checking social media when you have a moment of downtime, take a look around you. Simply ask yourself, "What would I do if . . ."

 . . . *someone walked in here right now brandishing a handgun?*
 . . . *I heard gunshots coming from behind that building?*
 . . . *that drunk guy tried to hug me?*

. . . this lady I'm beating at billiards decides to swing her cue at me after I sink the eight ball?

. . . I hurried into a truck-stop bathroom to relieve my bladder and there were some sketchy guys standing there?

This is a game you can never finish playing, and you can get better and quicker each time you play. You can also become more creative. The more you read, discuss, listen, and think, the better you will become. The ability you are developing makes you and everyone around you safer. Practicing this, making it a habit, is not just a prudent thing to do; it is morally virtuous. If you believe you have a moral responsibility to make the world, and the people in it, safer from harm and violence, then you should cultivate the ability to do so.

In playing this game, do not simply rely on your own musings. We need to learn from others. Fortunately, there are more authors today writing about this subject matter. Articles and books full of suggestions such as "if he does this, you beat him up in such and such a way" are still available, but they are now supplemented by more that address strategies for safety. Experts are available to share with us how to respond to danger in the most intelligent ways possible. These include discussions of recognizing types of violence, scaling of force, and the psychology of effective de-escalation. The bravado of many martial artists, detailing incidents where bad guys were vanquished, are being supplanted by stories of clever and creative methods to end violence without the use of more.

Ellis Amdur is an author, historian, and very large and capable martial artist. In *Dueling with O'Sensei* he writes about one incident he faced that could have ended very badly:

> One night, my then-wife and small child and I went to a movie in Ikebukero, a suburb of Tokyo. Afterwards, we went to a small park. She wanted to stretch her legs and do some *t'ai chi* after the show, so I was playing with my kid as she went through the form. Suddenly, from the shadows, I heard a muffled, "No! No! Let me go, someone, please . . ." I grabbed my son and placed him in my wife's arms and then moved quickly over to the dark corner of the park. A man was roughly pinning a woman to a bench, pawing at her, forcing kisses on her face, as she ineffectually struggled.
>
> [Would you have a plan to deal with this, at that very moment?]
>
> I said, "*Onichan* (a diminutive, a family term meaning, affectionately, "big brother;" also used ironically), you aren't being very nice."

He stayed on top of her as she struggled, yelling, "It's none of your business. Fuck off!"

"Onichan, it's not nice to pick on women when they don't want you to."

The man whirled and leapt to his feet. After hearing colloquial Japanese, his eyes widened to see me. I think he was also surprised because I don't think he had run into too many people taller than he was. Wearing a local university rugby jersey, he stood about 6 feet 4 inches and was thick as a brick. He raised a fist, and panting, told me again to leave them alone, it was none of my affair. Had I taken one of the many combat stances I had learned over the years, I think we would have started bouncing around the trees and stone benches at that instant.

I didn't, however. Strangely, I was not angry either. For some reason, it didn't seem necessary.

At any rate, hands still at my side, I looked at him in the eye like he was a younger version of myself and said, "Onichan, real men don't pick on girls, you know. 'S not right." We stood there without moving for the longest time. I could hear the young woman sobbing off to the side. I just looked in his eyes. I remember this sense of a kind of bubble surrounding us, a strange kind of quiet that was so full, so pregnant with meaning that it was almost tangible, and he picked up both fists, and in a calm way, almost in slow motion, I thought, "Here it comes," and I somehow relaxed still further, feeling like I could move in any direction, in any way I desired, and I kept looking gently into his eyes, and the moment continued to expand, and suddenly he exploded . . . in tears.[9]

Amdur finishes the account by explaining the backstory he discovered later: they were a young couple, and he really loved her but thought she cheated on him, and he just snapped. The story ends with Amdur and his family walking them to the train station, where the two parted ways.

It would be hard to script a better ending to what happened when Amdur discovered the scene in the park. The question for our purposes is, what made this possible? The hero in the story was not simply large and well-meaning—although those attributes probably helped. Amdur has spent his life cultivating physical and mental abilities to deal with dangerous and volatile situations. While big and strong, it was his extensive training in martial arts that allowed him to project a quiet strength and composure. Confidence allows one to remain calm, and this calmness is contagious. Amdur has also spent his professional life working in crisis intervention. He

9. Amdur, *Dueling With O'Sensei*, 235.

has developed the skills necessary to deescalate situations just like this one. Such a combination makes for great effectiveness in responding to violent and potentially violent encounters.

I suspect that the most well-meaning humanitarian, with a heart of gold but no such training, could not have achieved as positive a resolution to this conflict. Likewise, the most skilled and fearsome fighter would probably have failed to do so as well. In this case, both physical and mental facility worked together to resolve a very bad situation. We may never reach Amdur's level of expertise in the martial arts, or spend years working in crisis intervention, but we can all improve how we face violence. Wishing it so will not make it happen. Personal cultivation takes hard work.

CHAPTER 11

Cultivating Spirit

Pride is concerned with who is right. Humility is concerned with what is right.

—Ezra T. Benson

Possessing a strong body and mind are of paramount importance for the work of improving our communities. However, they are obviously not enough. The world has been full of vigorous and brilliant individuals who brought calamity on their nations and the world. As Dr. King wrote while still a student in college,

> The function of education, therefore, is to teach one to think intensively and to think critically. But education which stops with efficiency may prove the greatest menace to society. The most dangerous criminal may be the man gifted with reason, but with no morals . . . We must remember that intelligence is not enough. Intelligence plus character—that is the goal of true education.[1]

What is necessary is the cultivation of the spirit, the development of character, compassion, gratitude, and self-control. No less than the forging of the body and the schooling of the mind, this takes work.

A critical and coherent ethic of violence is important. Those who suffer from a conflicted morality struggle with many problems: poor decision-making, moral injury after the fact, and hesitation in the moment when

---

1. King, "Purpose of Education," paras. 4, 6.

action is needed. On the other hand, a clear ethical framework allows for quicker and more prudent decision-making. In those cases when violence may be required, "[W]hoever fights with a good and well-instructed conscience can also fight well."[2]

At the same time, holding a clear ethical position is no guarantee that we will act in accordance with our convictions. We human beings incline toward cowardliness, greed, and pride. These often stand in the way of acting in accordance with our principles. Clear ethical values may be essential, but they are not sufficient. Our spirit must be cultivated so that our own limitations and faults do not prevent us from living up to the ideals we espouse.

In many religious traditions, both eastern and western, we find tremendous resources for such spiritual cultivation. A thorough treatment of these is beyond the scope of this book, as their history and practice have existed around the globe for millennia. However, a few words may steer the reader in the right direction.

Mystical traditions in Judaism, Christianity, and Islam help adherents to attain oneness with God, a union where the mortal self finds and experiences the infinite. Protestantism focuses on the preaching of the gospel message of Christ, seeking to create gratitude to God which overflows in good works to one's neighbors. Muslims emphasize the "exertion" or "struggle" of *jihad*, first and foremost in one's internal efforts to overcome sin and improve one's own life for the service of God and community. Hinduism and Buddhism instruct their adherents along the way to overcoming illusion and attachment, thereby allowing our true nature to express itself in joy, peace, and compassion.

Returning to our narrow focus on the ethics of violence, and more specifically our concern with individual citizens within their communities, consider again the words of the Oracle of Delphi: "Know thyself." If we know our own strengths and weaknesses, desires and attachments, we are in a better position to address our faults. We are able to identify those facets of ourselves that prevent us from living up to the moral standards we set for ourselves.

Such a task is far from easy, as we often erect barriers to self-knowledge. We convince ourselves of the goodness of our character in order to avoid the unpleasant task of examining our flaws. Most people consider themselves pretty decent people, and so we do whatever is necessary to avoid the cognitive dissonance that arises from facing the realities of our actual selfishness, pettiness, and hubris. However, if my mother was right that "honesty is the best policy," then doing this uncomfortable work is yet another moral

2. Luther, "Whether Soldiers, Too, Can be Saved," 93.

imperative. Hauerwas was certainly correct when he wrote, "For violence is often the result of lies and half-truths we perpetrate on one another."[3] However, it is the "lies and half-truths" that we perpetrate on ourselves that very often keep us from real progress in moral development. There is an old Shinto saying that reads as follows: "To admit fault is the beginning of righteousness." Only with the recognition of sickness will we look for a cure.

With regard to our natural penchant for violence, we may begin with a saying that is popular among teachers of Okinawan karate: *Iji ga detara te o hiki; te ga detara iji o hiki*; that is, "If your temper rises, withdraw your hand; if your hand rises, withdraw your temper."[4] The following question presents itself, then: what prompts your temper to rise? What gets under your skin and makes you lose it? The reader will recall from chapter 7 that Thomas Aquinas argues that what turns legitimate self-defense into the mortal sin of "brawling" is when it is motivated by anger.[5] Without the knowledge of what stokes our temper, anger, or even rage, it is impossible to cultivate our character and behavior.

Adherents of nonviolence in traditions like Hinduism and Buddhism teach that it is impossible for violent acts to follow from an enlightened mind. Gandhi taught, "Violence is simply not possible unless one is driven by anger, by ignorant love and by hatred. The Gīta, on the other hand, wants us to be incapable of anger."[6] One need not agree with Gandhi that all violence comes from anger and hatred to recognize that a great deal does. Thus, identifying what prompts such emotions in us is essential to cultivating a spirit that is in control of when "your hand rises."

Years ago, I had a student in my karate class who was prone to losing his temper. What really forced an emotional reaction in him, it turned out, was if someone put a finger in his face. For most of us, if someone invades our personal space and literally sticks a finger in our face, we experience a few emotions: indignation, annoyance, anger, frustration. These emotions can lead us to make foolish decisions. However, if such an incident prompts something closer to rage, the potential for truly dangerous consequences is present, for everyone around. Thus, first identifying this trigger, and then

3. Hauerwas, *Peaceable Kingdom*, 133.

4. Higaonna, *History of Karate*, 115.

5. Aquinas, *Summa Theologica* 2a2æ 41, 1.

6. As in Gier, *Virtue of Nonviolence*, 37. This idea is not unique to the East. English Quaker James Naylor (1616–1660) in *The Lamb's War* (1657) was among the first to teach that all fighting stems from selfishness and pride. Those who can eliminate pride will be unable to engage in violent acts toward others (Chernus, "Religion and Nonviolence," 554–67).

working to limit the emotional reaction to it, was essential for him fostering intelligent resolutions to potentially violent situations.

My friend Gottfried has a different but related emotional trigger. For him, it is being publicly disrespected. We generally dislike when others treat us disrespectfully. However, when it becomes a particularly potent "button" for a person, it must be addressed. Prideful overreactions to such an affront lead to untold fighting and killing around the world every day. Apologizing to a bully for a perceived slight is hard, but it is sometimes the wise thing to do. Cooperating with a police officer who is berating—and possibly arresting—you for no good reason is the right thing to do, even if it takes every ounce of self-control to do so. Justice can be sought later, but that is cold comfort to a young man trying to hold on to his dignity and reputation, especially in front of his friends. When a police officer or civilian has a chip on his shoulder, any contention between the two of them can tend to be problematic. When they both have that chip, things can easily turn quite ugly. Knowing that disrespect triggers strong emotions, again, is the first step. Laboring to rein in those passions is the work that must follow.

Pride

While the individual triggers vary, there is often a common underlying cause: pride. It is pride, according to many western religions, that is a "special" kind of sin. In Judaism, the sin of pride is often spoken against in the scriptures: "Pride goes before destruction, and a haughty spirit before a fall."[7] Yahweh himself models modesty, choosing to speak to Moses from a lowly bush, and coming down to the smallest of mountains (Mount Sinai) to deliver the Law. And while human beings may be the crowning achievement of creation, they should always remember their place. Thus, the Hasidic rabbi Simcha Bunim (1765–1827) recommended placing two slips of paper in one's pockets—one of which reads "I am dust and ashes"; the other, "For my sake the world was created." These must forever be balanced.

Christianity has often viewed pride as the root sin of all others sins. In addition to the Old Testament prohibitions, Christians interpret the fall of Adam and Eve as a result of pride, wanting to be like God. Jesus, the Son of God, is born of human flesh in a cave where people normally kept animals. The great saving act of God was accomplished with Jesus hung on a tree and executed. Over the centuries, Christians have focused on pride and how it leads to numerous other sins, including unjust violence. Pope Gregory I (c. 540–604 AD) taught, "Pride is by no means content with the destruction of

7. Prov 16:18.

one virtue; it raises itself up against all the powers of the soul, and like an all-pervading and poisonous disease corrupts the whole body."[8] Thomas Aquinas quotes Gregory[9] and then goes on to say, "Boasting and self-inflation, the results of pride or vainglory, do not cause quarrels or brawls directly; but they can be occasions."[10] It is not only fear that can lead to anger, hate, and suffering. Pride causes nation to rise against nation, spouse against spouse, and neighbor against neighbor. If one is to live a virtuous life, seeking to minimize violence, it is necessary to tame one's pride.[11]

Likewise, Islam contains numerous prohibitions against pride, which is considered one of the greatest sins. Satan fell because of pride. The Koran teaches, "Certainly [Allah] does not love the proud ones" (16:23). In the oral tradition of the *Hadith* it is said, "Whosoever has in his heart, even an atom of pride he will not enter paradise." Muslims who go on pilgrimage to Mecca must remain in a state of ritual purity and modesty known as *ihram*. Men wear simple clothing that consists of two unhemmed sheets, so that all are equal and no one seeks pride of place because of their attire.

Pride as a primary cause of violence is not only intuitive, but is supported by empirical evidence. In her book *More Moral Than God: Taking Responsibility for Religious Violence*, Charlene Burns examines the research that shows which personality types are more prone to violence. It turns out that people with a penchant for violence tend to have high (but unstable) self-esteem. It is not those who merely think highly of themselves, or have objective reasons for their lofty self-assessment, but those who have a strong desire to see themselves as superior to others, regardless of the evidence. That is to say, people who experience a strong need to feel superior to others are more prone to violence. Burns explains, "They consciously believe that they are superior to others, and this sense of superiority is not grounded in objective reality. Baseless, and therefore fragile, high self-esteem is a strong predictor of violence and aggression."[12] The research also shows a correlation between narcissism and both serial killers and rapists.

This observation is not only relevant for those individuals who are narcissistic. While you and I may not be textbook narcissists, egotism exists on

---

8. Gregory, *Moral* xxxiv, 23, as cited in Aquinas, *Summa Theologica* 2a2æ 162, 2.

9. Aquinas, *Summa Theologica* 2a2æ 162, 2.

10. Aquinas, *Summa Theologica* 2a2æ 41, 2, ad. 2.

11. Decades ago, there were some feminists who argued that the fundamental sin of women is different than that of men (e.g., Saiving, "Human Situation"). Men may struggle with pride, but women tend to sin by not actualizing their God-given potential. I believe that this position is based on a very limited notion of what Augustine and others meant by "pride."

12. Burns, *More Moral Than God*, 73. See also Baumeister, *Evil*.

a scale. Many of us exhibit traits of this personality type from time to time. We can all demonstrate narcissism in our lives without being paradigmatic narcissists. Thus, while most of us do not suffer from extreme egotism or have inclinations toward murder, we are all subject to hubris, or pride, and the predisposition toward unjust violence that it can create. Working to unseat pride is then a necessary component in working to control predilections for violence.

Making a decision to stop being prideful is, quite obviously, not sufficient. Jews, Muslims, and Christians have long sought to combat this common human weakness. They have taught and practiced a variety of approaches to help their adherents make progress in this regard.

The examples of Yahweh, Moses, and Jesus above are often cited. Muhammad lived a simple and modest life in many ways, and reportedly said, "I do not like to be treated as if I were privileged because God does not like any of His creatures to consider himself privileged or to be treated as if he were privileged over others."

Whether one looks to the moral paradigm of the Buddha, Jesus, Muhammad, Gandhi, or Mother Teresa, the example of humility is a powerful antidote to pride. We find such individuals throughout history, literature, and even our own families or neighborhoods. Finding a model is an important start. Becoming such an example is how *shalom/salaam* is truly cultivated.

One of the most respected karate teachers in the world today is Morio Higaonna. Those who train with him always remark on both his incredible ability and his remarkable humility. Having had the privilege of spending some time with him myself, I can say that he inspires his students not only to be better martial artists, but better human beings. His own teacher inspired him in the same way. "He taught me that one should always seek humility and that the stronger one becomes the more humble one should be. He likened this to a stalk of rice which bends lower as it grows taller."[13]

In addition to the people who inspire us, who we seek to emulate, many religious traditions encourage particular practices that are also designed to cultivate humility and chase away pride. Ascetic disciplines, like fasting, can be found in the majority of world religions, in addition to other more severe disciplines. Self-flagellation in Shi'a Islam and reenactments of the crucifixion among Filipino Catholics are more extreme expressions of this.[14] Meditation on the corrupt nature of humanity or the grace of God,

---

13. Higaonna, *History of Karate*, 155. Incidentally, I once heard Kazuo Terauchi, one of Higaonna's most senior students and a frighteningly powerful man, teach the same exact thing at a training seminar in Annapolis, MD.

14. It is important to point out, however, that excelling in ascetic practices can

likewise, seeks to combat hubris. Among the mystics, efforts to lose oneself in communion with the divine may achieve the same end.

Each religion has its own theology and practices to help overcome the human propensity for pride. When we observe the near-universality of these disciplines of spiritual cultivation, we begin to understand how important human beings have regarded such work. Whether we avail ourselves of them, of course, is up to us.

Ignorance

If western religions emphasize *pride* as a root cause of many other evils, eastern traditions place more weight on the dangers of *ignorance*. The reason for the suffering we create in the world is often grounded in ignorance. The nature of this problem varies in different religions, as does the prescription for its cure. However, we can identify a few common threads that run through these traditions, and discuss how overcoming ignorance permits us to address situations of violence in our world more effectively.

Illusion

When Hindus speak of this world as "illusion" (*maya*), they do not typically mean that the earth and we who live on it are not real. Rather, it is our perception of ourselves, and our place in the universe, that is flawed. Human beings tend to think of themselves as individual things in the world, separate from other things in the world, and distinct from the Divine (*Brahman*). The truth, according to this tradition, is that there is actually a fundamental connection between all living beings and *Brahman*.

According to Swami Vivekananda (1863–1902), "The *Vedas* [Hindu scriptures] cannot show you Brahman, you are that already. They can only help to take away the veil that hides truth from our eyes. The cessation of ignorance can only come when I know that God and I are one."[15] If, then, we are all one with the divine, it follows that we are all one with one another. However, we suffer from this illusion that we are all separate and unconnected. When we come to appreciate our unity, our common origin and destiny, then we can no longer view one another as enemies. Unfortunately, we all suffer from the same ignorance, the same illusions. We hurt ourselves

become its own source of pride.

15. Vivekananda, *Inspired Talks*, 73.

and others because of this. The recognition of our essential interconnectedness keeps us from the hatred that drives violence to ever-increasing levels.

When I was a young boy, I remember sitting and pondering a very important question: is everyone else just like me? That is to say, does everyone on earth feel the same strength of emotions, have the same intensity of fears, enjoy the same excitement of pleasure, and ponder such questions with the same depth of feeling?[16] If so, I need to treat everyone with the same decency that I want to receive from them! Four decades later, I believe this intuition I had as a boy was likely the most important insight I have ever had. Perhaps it is the most we can hope for.

At the same time, I recognized then what I still perceive today: I am incapable of actually perceiving the full humanity of everyone I meet. Every person I pass in the mall, I am unable to perceive them as possessing the same depth of humanity that I possess. With regard to my neighbors, co-workers, and certainly the people I dislike, I do not recognize in them the same value as a human being that I perceive in myself. Even with my close friends and family, I am not capable of seeing the fullness of who they are and what they experience.

One need not be a Hindu and accept the philosophy of *Brahman* in order to recognize our unity as human beings. Monotheists should reach a similar conclusion: all people are created by God and share "the image and likeness" of their Creator. The question is whether one will work to cultivate a greater awareness, a personally appropriated recognition of the truth that all human beings possess the same immeasurable value.

Different religions teach various methods to achieve this. Whether one pursues this through meditation, the reading of scriptures, purposeful listening to others, or the deliberate effort to remind oneself of others' full humanity, it is essential work for those who strive to live a life according to the Golden Rule. It is necessary as an impetus to work toward *shalom/salaam* in our world.

Attachment

In Buddhism, there is a doctrine known as the Twelve *Nidānas*, which explains the chain of cause and effect that creates misery, prevents enlightenment, and perpetuates rebirth in this world of suffering.[17] This causal sequence begins with *avidyā* (ignorance). While Buddhism teaches that we

---

16. The word "sonder" is sometimes given to this realization.

17. The twelve are: ignorance, mental formations, consciousness, name/form, six senses, contact, feelings, craving, grasping, becoming, birth, aging and death.

are ignorant of many things (e.g., the nature of our true self, the cause of suffering), much of our ignorance boils down to the issue of attachment. We do not perceive how our attachment to things, ideas, categories, and even our "self," contributes to the ongoing suffering in our lives and in our world.

Human beings commit acts of violence when they want something they do not have. They fight each other when they fear someone will take something from them. Sometimes these "things" are physical, like money or possessions. Sometimes they are more abstract, like honor or status. In reality, Buddhism teaches, there is nothing we can truly possess. Everything is temporary, from our possessions to our relationships, even our own existence. When we attach ourselves to things and people, as if they were ours to keep forever, we create suffering when they are taken from us. Sometimes we harm others; sometimes we harm ourselves.

This realization is not unique to Buddhists. Hauerwas writes, "For our possessions are the source of our violence."[18] However, Buddhism has developed this insight to a more sophisticated and profound level. We attach to ideologies, categories, and philosophies, as if they could encapsulate the essence of our "empty" cosmos. This attachment carries over to the concept of our very self. We attach to the idea that we have a permanent, fixed identity which we must fight to preserve in this world and the next. These attachments perpetuate suffering and keep us from compassion. Only when we realize that our reality is empty of any fixed substance, can we begin to loosen our grip on the things of this world. Only then can we be at peace with the changing vicissitudes of life.

Ueshiba taught, "If you have not linked yourself to true emptiness, you will never understand the Art of Peace."[19] The Rinzai Zen master Taisen Deshimaru taught a similar principle to his students who were also martial artists. "In the martial arts, too, one must be *mushotoku*, without any goal or desire for profit."[20] Craving after recognition, honors, respect, and power are completely at odds with what Ueshiba called the "Art of Peace." Attachments to such "achievements" often corrupt the nature of martial artists, so that the tools they are developing are more likely to be used to create suffering, rather than alleviate it.

Twenty years ago in Nashville, I had a little road rage incident which led to another driver following me through the streets. I pulled over in a public place with lots of witnesses. As we both exited our vehicles, he walked

18. Hauerwas, *Peaceable Kingdom*, 86.

19. As in Raposa, *Meditation and the Martial Arts*, 31. Ueshiba was not actually a Buddhist. He belonged to a religious sect known as Ōmoto-kyō. Nevertheless, this statement clearly shows the influence of Buddhist thought on his philosophy.

20. Deshimaru, *Zen Way to the Martial Arts*, 38.

over, threatening to do me bodily harm. I calmly explained that there was plenty of blame to go around, that I did not want to fight, but that I would "drop him on his ass" if he started anything. I do not know if it was the best response for that situation, but it seemed to work. He repeated his overwrought complaint about my behavior, and I repeated my reply. At that point, he seemed satisfied that he had made his point, and things were wrapping up. However, realizing that I had successfully defused the situation, I started making verbal jabs back at him. I did not want simply to walk away unharmed—I wanted to win. I was craving some sort of victory, a feeling of triumph. There was some ideal of masculinity in my mind that I wanted to attain. Needless to say, things started heating up again. I stopped needling him, and once again things calmed down. After he left, I asked myself, "Why did you do that?" It was a foolish thing to do that could have triggered completely unnecessary violence.

So, why *did* I do that? I suppose it was a desire to win, a craving for dominance, indignation at him for starting the whole situation, and wanting to feel secure in my masculinity. In other words, there were a number of "things" I wanted to possess. I was too attached to ideas and images, feelings and ego, and I almost prompted a violent encounter because of it—even after I had first demonstrated the maturity and ability to de-escalate the situation.

Fortunately, there are ways to overcome our attachments and craving. Buddhists have a vast array of teachings and practices to do so. At the same time, they understand that cultivation of the spirit is tremendously difficult. It takes many years of work. Nevertheless, every reduction in our attachments and desires contributes to greater compassion and less suffering in the world. The road requires great effort, mindfulness, and concentration, but we can make progress in this direction.

The learning of contentment is not the purview of Buddhists alone. Many non-Buddhists make use of Buddhist meditation and literary resources to achieve the same end. In fact, any practice that cultivates such a spirit is useful. Recognition of our attachments, which are very often the result of our pride and ignorance, is an essential place to start. Overcoming these deficiencies is hard work, but the contributions of religious leaders, philosophers (n.b. the Stoics!), therapists, and motherly advice are available to us if we are willing to engage what they offer.

An individual's ethic of violence must aim for fidelity to good moral principles and the creation of a just peace. Yet, as we have seen, that is not enough. Many limitations exist that stand in the way of actually living out the principles we espouse. A physical inability to fight or flee reduces the number of options we have in a violent encounter. A lack of knowledge regarding the nature of violence prevents us from responding to it intelligently. Lastly, even with physical ability and a good game plan, we can easily create more harm than good if our actions are governed by pride, illusion, and ignorance. Cultivation of the spirit is no less important—and perhaps more important!—than knowledge and skill.

Throughout this book, I have argued that violence is a tool that can be used for good or harm. Though often a dreadful act, it need not be regarded universally as a moral failing or essentially corrupt action. Nevertheless, it is a particularly powerful tool that generates consequences that extend far beyond its immediate use. Violence may be advisable, even if it is at the same time lamentable.

With regard to that terrible moral choice that we all hope we are spared, I return to the insight of Ellis Amdur. "Is there any self-defense or justifiable homicide? Of course there is, but a part of the justification lies in having striven with every fiber of one's being to never be in such a position that one is forced to take a life."[21] Without that striving, there can be no moral virtue in violence.

21. Amdur, *Dueling with O'Sensei*, 257.

Bibliography

Ali, Mohamed M., and Iqbal H. Shah. "Sanctions and Childhood Mortality in Iraq." *The Lancet* 355 (2000) 1851–57.

Ambrose of Milan. *Of the Duties of the Clergy.* London: Aeterna, 2016.

Amdur, Ellis. *Dueling with O'Sensei: Grappling with the Myth of the Warrior Sage.* Wheaton, IL: Freelance Academy, 2015

———. *Old School: Essays on Japanese Martial Traditions.* Wheaton, IL: Freelance Academy, 2013.

Aquinas, Thomas. *Summa Theologica: Translated by Fathers of the English Dominican Province.* London: Burns, Oates, and Washbourne, 1916.

Baer, H. David. *Recovering Christian Realism: Just War Theory as a Political Ethic.* Lanham, MD: Lexington, 2015.

Bartholomeusz, Tessa. "In Defense of Dharma: Just-War Ideology in Buddhist Sri Lanka." *Journal of Buddhist Ethics* 6 (1999) 1–16.

Baumeister, Roy F. *Evil: Inside Human Violence and Cruelty.* New York: Holt, 1999.

Bazargan, Saba. "Varieties of Contingent Pacifism in War." In *How We Fight: Ethics in War,* edited by Helen Frowe and Gerald Lang, 1–17. Oxford: Oxford University Press, 2014.

Brimlow, Robert W. *What About Hitler? Wrestling with Jesus's Call to Nonviolence in an Evil World.* Grand Rapids: Brazos, 2006.

Burns, Charlene. *More Moral Than God: Taking Responsibility for Religious Violence.* Lanham, MD: Rowman and Littlefield, 2008.

Carlson, John D. "Religion and Violence: Coming to Terms with Terms." In *The Blackwell Companion to Religion and Violence,* edited by Andrew R. Murphy, 7–22. Chichester: Wiley-Blackwell, 2011.

Chapple, Christopher Key. "The Dialectic of Violence in Jainism." In *The Blackwell Companion to Religion and Violence,* edited by Andrew R. Murphy, 263–70. Chichester, UK: Wiley-Blackwell, 2011.

Chernus, Ira. "Religion and Nonviolence in American History." In *The Blackwell Companion to Religion and Violence,* edited by Andrew R. Murphy, 554–67. Chichester, UK: Wiley-Blackwell, 2011.

Confucius. *The Analects of Confucius.* Translated by Arthur Waley. New York: Vintage, 1938.

Dear, John. "To Kill or Not to Kill: Just War or Nonviolence?" Lecture presented at College of Mount Saint Vincent, Bronx, NY, April 4, 2017. https://vimeo.com/232078835.

Demiéville, Paul. "Buddhism and War." In *Buddhist Warfare*, edited by Michael K. Jerryson and Mark Juergensmeyer, 17–57. Oxford: Oxford University Press, 2010.

Deshimaru, Taisen. *The Zen Way to the Martial Arts*. New York: Compass, 1982.

Dundas, Paul. *The Jains*. The Library of Religious Beliefs and Practices. 2nd ed. New York: Routledge, 2002.

Funakoshi, Gichin. *Karate-Do: My Way of Life*. New York: Kodansha, 1975.

Gethin, Rupert. "Can Killing a Living Being Ever Be an Act of Compassion? The Analysis of the Act of Killing in the Abhidharma and Pali Commentaries." *Journal of Buddhist Ethics* 11 (2004) 167–202.

Gier, Nicholas F. *The Virtue of Nonviolence: From Gautama to Gandhi*. New York: State University of New York Press, 2004.

Goldberg, Jonah. "Softheaded Moralizing at School." *USA Today*, September 1, 2015.

Golinski, Matthias. "Conversations with Franz Bork: Karate Needs Perseverance." *Classical Fighting Arts* 3.1 (2015) 53–62.

Grossman, David. *On Killing: The Psychological Cost of Learning to Kill in War and Society*. Boston: Little, Brown and Co., 1995.

Grotius, Hugo. *On the Law of War and Peace*. Edited by Stephen C. Neff. Student edition. Cambridge: Cambridge University Press, 2012.

Harvey, Peter. *An Introduction to Buddhism: Teachings, History and Practices*. Cambridge: Cambridge University Press, 1990.

Hauerwas, Stanley. *The Peaceable Kingdom: A Primer In Christian Ethics*. Notre Dame: Notre Dame Press, 1983.

Higaonna, Morio. *The History of Karate: Okinawan Goju-Ryu*. West Meon, UK: Dragon, 1995.

Jacobs, Mark. "The Man Who Never Was." *Black Belt*, December 2013.

Jenkins, Stephen. "Making Merit through Warfare and Torture According to the Ārya-Bidhisattva-gocara-upāyavisaya-vikurvana-nirdeśa *Sūtra*." In *Buddhist Warfare*, edited by Michael K. Jerryson and Mark Juergensmeyer, 59–75. Oxford: Oxford University Press, 2010.

Jerryson, Michael K. "Introduction." In *Buddhist Warfare*, edited by Michael K. Jerryson and Mark Juergensmeyer, 3–16. Oxford: Oxford University Press, 2010.

John Paul II. "Address to the International Conference on Nutrition." *Origins* 22 (1992) 475.

Johnson, James Turner. *Ethics and the Use of Force: Just War in Historical Perspective*. Burlington: Ashgate, 2011.

———. *The Quest for Peace: Three Moral Traditions in Western Cultural History*. Princeton: Princeton University Press, 1987.

Kane, Lawrence A., and Kris Wilder. *The Little Black Book of Violence*. Wolfeboro, NH: YMAA, 2009.

Keown, Damien. *Buddhist Ethics: A Very Short Introduction*. Oxford: Oxford University Press, 2005.

Kershaw, Alex. *The Liberator: One World War II Soldier's 500-Day Odyssey From the Beaches of Sicily to the Gates of Dachau*. New York: Crown, 2012.

King, Martin Luther, Jr. "The Purpose of Education." *The Maroon Tiger*, January–February, 1947.

Kudo, Timothy. "I Killed People in Afghanistan. Was I Right or Wrong?" *The Washington Post*, January 25, 2013. https://www.washingtonpost.com/opinions/i-killed-people-in-afghanistan-was-i-right-or-wrong/2013/01/25/c0b0d5a6-60ff-11e2-b05a-605528f6b712_story.html?noredirect=on&utm_term=.b12d1f1f4799.

Lackey, Douglas P. "Pacifism." In *Contemporary Moral Problems: War and Terrorism*, edited by James E. White, 7–21. Belmont, CA: Wadsworth, 2006.

Lang, Gerald. "Why Not Forfeiture?" In *How We Fight: Ethics in War*, edited by Helen Frowe and Gerald Lang, 38–61. Oxford: Oxford University Press, 2014.

Lee, Steven P. *Ethics and War: An Introduction*. Cambridge Applied Ethics. New York: Cambridge University Press, 2012.

Litz, Brett T., et al. "Moral Injury and Moral Repair in War Veterans: A Preliminary Model and Intervention Strategy." *Clinical Psychology Review* 29 (2009) 695–706.

Locke, John. *The Second Treatise of Government*. New York: Liberal Arts, 1952.

Luther, Martin. "Against the Robbing and Murdering Hordes of Peasants." In *Christian in Society III*, edited by Helmut T. Lehmann and Robert C. Schultz, 45–56. Vol. 46 of *Luther's Works*. Philadelphia: Fortress, 1967.

———. "Whether Soldiers, Too, Can Be Saved." In *Christian in Society III*, edited by Helmut T. Lehmann and Robert C. Schultz, 87–138. Vol. 46 of *Luther's Works*. Philadelphia: Fortress, 1967.

Maher, Derek F. "Sacralized Warfare: The Fifth Dalai Lama and the Discourse of Religious Violence." In *Buddhist Warfare*, edited by Michael K. Jerryson and Mark Juergensmeyer, 77–90. Oxford: Oxford University Press, 2010.

Mann, Jeffrey K. "Luther on Reason: What Makes a Whore a Whore." *Seminary Ridge Review* 18 (2015) 1–17.

———. "Lutherans in Need of Self-Discipline: Japanese *Shugyō* and the Art of Sanctification." *Dialog: A Journal of Theology* 50.3 (2011) 271–79.

———. *When Buddhists Attack: The Curious Relationship Between Zen and the Martial Arts*. Rutland, VT: Tuttle, 2012.

McMahan, Jeff. *Killing in War*. Uehiro Series in Practical Ethics. Reprint. Oxford: Oxford University Press, 2011.

Meagher, Robert Emmet. *Killing from the Inside Out: Moral Injury and Just War*. Eugene, OR: Cascade, 2014.

Metaxas, Eric. *Bonhoeffer: Pastor, Martyr, Prophet, Spy*. Nashville: Nelson, 2010.

Miller, Rory. *Meditations on Violence*. Wolfeboro, NH: YMAA, 2008.

———. *Training for Sudden Violence: 72 Practical Drills*. Wolfeboro, NH: YMAA, 2016.

Miller, Rory, and Lawrence A. Kane. *Scaling Force: Dynamic Decision-Making Under Threat of Violence*. Wolfeboro, NH: YMAA, 2012.

National Conference of Catholic Bishops. "Harvest of Justice is Sown in Peace." http://www.usccb.org/beliefs-and-teachings/what-we-believe/catholic-social-teaching/the-harvest-of-justice-is-sown-in-peace.cfm.

Niebuhr, Reinhold. *An Interpretation of Christian Ethics*. New York: Harper & Row, 1935.

———. *Moral Man and Immoral Society*. New York: Charles Scribner's Sons, 1960.

O'Donovan, Oliver. *The Just War Revisited*. Current Issues in Theology. Cambridge: Cambridge University Press, 2003.

Otake, Risuke. *The Deity and the Sword: Katori Shintō Ryū, Vol. 1*. Tokyo: Japan Publications, 1977.

Palmer, Harold. *Christian Pacifism and Just War Theory: Discipleship and the Ethics of War, Violence and the Use of Force*. N.p.: Logos Light, 2016.

Pojman, Louis P. *Ethics: Discovering Right and Wrong*. Belmont, CA: Wadsworth, 2002.

Raposa, Michael L. *Meditation and the Martial Arts.* Charlottesville: University of Virginia Press, 2013.

"Report: Average Male 4,000% Less Effective In Fights Than They Imagine." https://https://www.theonion.com/report-average-male-4-000-less-effective-in-fights-th-1819576624.

Saiving, Valerie. "The Human Situation: A Feminine View." *The Journal of Religion* 40 (1960) 100–12.

Shahar, Meir. *The Shaolin Monastery: History, Religion, and the Chinese Martial Arts.* Honolulu: University of Hawai'i Press, 2008.

Stendahl, Krister. *Roots of Violence: Creating Peace Through Spiritual Reconciliation.* Brewster, MA: Paraclete, 2016.

Stevens, John. *The Philosophy of Aikido.* New York: Kodansha International, 2001.

Tankosich, Mark J. "Karate ni Sente Nashi: What the Masters Had to Say." *Hiroshima University of Economics Journal of Humanities, Social and Natural Sciences* 27.1 (2004) 1–7.

Uniacke, Suzanne. "Self-Defence, Just War, and a Reasonable Prospect of Success." In *How We Fight: Ethics in War,* edited by Helen Frowe and Gerald Lang, 62–74. Oxford: Oxford University Press, 2014.

Victoria, Brian A. *Zen at War.* New York: Weatherhill, 1997.

———. *Zen War Stories.* New York: RoutledgeCurzon, 2003.

Vivekananda, Swami. *Inspired Talks, My Master and Other Writings.* Vol. 7 of *The Complete Works of Swami Vivekananda.* New York: Ramakrishna-Vivekananda Center, 1976.

Waller, James. *Becoming Evil: How Ordinary People Commit Genocide and Mass Killings.* Oxford: Oxford University Press, 2002.

Walzer, Michael. *Just and Unjust Wars: A Moral Argument With Historical Illustrations.* 3rd ed. New York: Basic, 1977.

Yoder, John H. *What Would You Do? A Serious Answer to a Standard Question.* Exp. ed. Scottsdale, PA: Herald, 1992.

Young, Robert. "Hayward Nishioka Reveals How Judo Changed His Life—And How It Can Change Yours!" *Black Belt,* June 24, 2013.

Printed in the USA
CPSIA information can be obtained
at www.ICGtesting.com
LVHW051244271124
797764LV00002B/138

9 781532 652035